DESPERATE
MEASURES

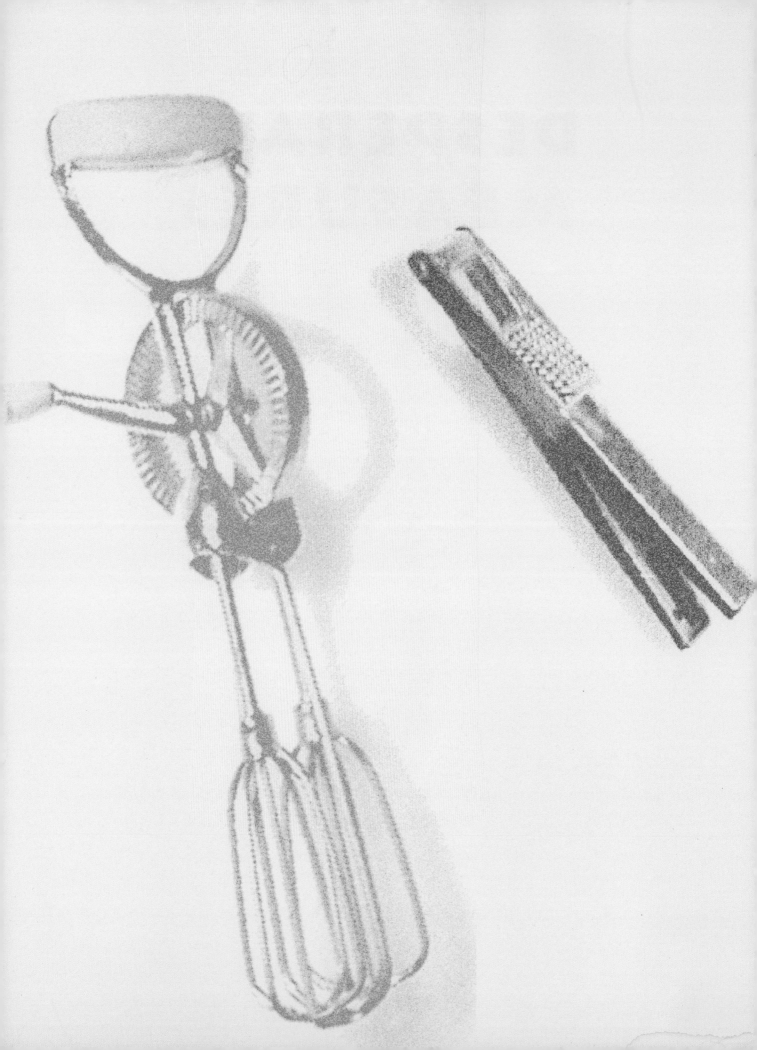

DESPERATE
MEASURES

90 UNINTIMIDATING
RECIPES FOR THE
DOMESTICALLY INEPT

KEVIN CRAFTS

PHOTOGRAPHS BY JOSHUA GREENE

CLARKSON POTTER/PUBLISHERS

NEW YORK

✳

FOR HELEN
AND CLIFF

✳

Published by Clarkson N. Potter, Inc., 201 East 50th Street, New York, New York 10022. Member of the Crown Publishing Group.

Random House, Inc. New York, Toronto, London, Sydney, Auckland

CLARKSON N. POTTER, POTTER, and colophon are trademarks of Clarkson N. Potter, Inc.

Manufactured in Hong Kong

Design by Altemus Creative Servicenter

Library of Congress
Cataloging-in-Publication Data
Crafts, Kevin.
Desperate measures: 90 unintimidating recipes for the domestically inept/by Kevin Crafts; photographs by Joshua Greene.
1. Cookery. I. Title.
TX714.C725 1993   92-7503
641.5—dc20   CIP
ISBN 0-517-88009-1

10   9   8   7   6   5   4   3   2   1
First Edition

ACKNOWLEDGMENTS

Clearly, the greatest benefit to working on a book like this is the people you meet and the friends you make along the way. With that in mind I would like to thank those people who made this book as much a dream as a reality:

Joshua Greene and his crew, Carl J. Horner, Soffie Gryzbowskie, Marco Ricca, and Bobby Sanchez, for providing not only the photographs but also humor and advice, constructive or otherwise, all along the way. I hope that you all had as much fun as I did. I know you ate well.

My assistants: Marissa Iavarone, for always being there with a shoulder, a cigarette, and her very infectious laughter at all the right moments; Garvin Burke, for cracking the proverbial whip and keeping things moving in a fashion that is truly his own; and Julia Pemberton, for her storytelling as well as her culinary skills.

Glenn Marziali: This book would not have been possible if not for your infinite patience, kindness and honesty, constant love and support, and a really spectacular scallop recipe.

Both of my families—the Crafts, Cliff and Eileen; and the Marzialis, Aris and Ninette—for sharing their love of foods both American and European and all the memories that go with them.

Lee Bailey, Mary Emmerling, and Tricia Foley, for not only setting such stellar examples, but for so aptly answering all the questions I was too embarrassed to ask anyone else.

Everyone who opened their homes to us and allowed us to create mayhem where once there was order: Mary Foley and Kirby Redding, Tim Herr, Rosemary, Bill, and Claudia Culhane.

My agent, Gayle Benderoff, for always looking out for me.

My friends at Clarkson Potter: Lauren Shakely, for introducing order to my life; Dana Earlenbaugh and Kristin Frederickson, for organizational skills that would scare Katherine Gibbs; Catherine Sustana; designer Robert Altemus; art director Howard Klein; production editor Mark McCauslin; and production manager Joan Denman.

And finally to those who filled in the gaps with a recipe, a story, or a cloth napkin: Brana Amsel Buzel; Margaret Fey; Rosemary Haynes Oberndorf; Grace Lawlor; my aunt, M. L. Scanlon; and my illustrious sister, Kathy Crafts-Belair.

✳ CONTENTS ✳

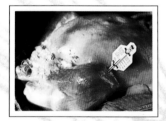

INTRODUCTION

Granted, at first it's a horrible thought: The doorbell rings and beyond wait friends you know far too well to threaten with your Doritos y Dip one more time. If they are polite, they might subject themselves to a few obligatory bites and then inquire about a possible pizza delivery, or maybe just suffer silently as the imitation cheese food solidifies on the otherwise naked chips. But why test the eternal bonds of friendship? Chances are that you are far more resourceful than you think and that only a lack of self-confidence separates you and your guests from a self-cooked repast that any respectable eatery would be proud to serve. Stop thinking of popcorn as a side dish and rise to the occasion.

As a free-lance food stylist for the past several years, I have earned my living putting together unbelievable meals with the aid of more weapons from the batterie de cuisine than I care to remember. But I have also learned how to make the same incredible meals possible for those of us with great aspirations and realistic appetites (and real kitchens).

Cooking began for me during my poverty-stricken undergraduate days, when I lived on a diet of coffee, French fries, and macaroni and cheese from a box. After college, I graduated to chicken parts with lemon pepper and soy sauce, accompanied by a medley of frozen broccoli, cauliflower, and carrots. It wasn't until I had taken a few short courses in cooking—

one that taught me how to make turtles and alligators out of cucumbers and bunnies out of olives (skills I'm sure never to use or to forget)—that my interest in food and cooking developed beyond the hobby stage. As an art school graduate, I also took an interest in the way food looked.

Now, working with a diversity of foods on as daily a basis as I can manage, I can weed out the foods that are too difficult and too time-consuming to consider. The food I make around the house is low-effort and low-key: rice, basic salads, and pasta—perhaps an occasional bowtie fagioli, but no more macaroni and cheese from a box. My aim in writing this book was to skip fancy foods and show you how to make really good food using basic ingredients and simple techniques that should be familiar to anyone who has passed through the kitchen on the way to the dining room. These menus can all be prepared after just one trip to the market and a very sincere attempt in the kitchen.

I am not going to explain what flour is or how to boil water, and I won't be handing down the Ten Commandments of Entertaining. The recipes I have included here are the ones that have worked most successfully for me, a fellow nonchef. Since I am intimidated by ingredients that take up half the kitchen or require a chemistry degree to handle safely, I've kept the list of foods to a very important few, with only a couple of exceptions. And I have eliminated all recipes that require so much energy that they cease to be any fun. Believe it or not, entertaining is supposed to be fun. Trying to emulate the picture you have just torn out of your favorite foreign magazine is no way to overcome a fear of entertaining. Avoid guides that require your allegiance to several days in the kitchen until you know that the kitchen is really where you want to spend your

time. Finally, start taking advantage of your local supermarket. Upon closer inspection, you will find that supermarkets stock spices and unusual vegetables that until a few years ago were available only in big city specialty shops.

Confidence is the most important kitchen tool. If something doesn't rise, gel, or whip the way you think it should, just move on, improvise, or take a deep breath and start over. Don't get excited or belittle yourself. Not only does hysteria get in the way of the task at hand, but it can also destroy any atmosphere you had hoped to create. Encourage yourself with the thought of six to eight very impressed friends, groaning with full stomachs, licking their plates more efficiently than any dog in the neighborhood, and begging for more.

Even though you probably had M & M's for breakfast several times this week and your favorite ashtray may also be your best serving dish, you can still serve a really great meal at home just this once. If—and this only happens once in a lifetime—you produce nothing fit for human consumption, remember: given the right situation, cuisine can be as simple as coffee and a cigarette. ◾

DESPERATE MEASURES

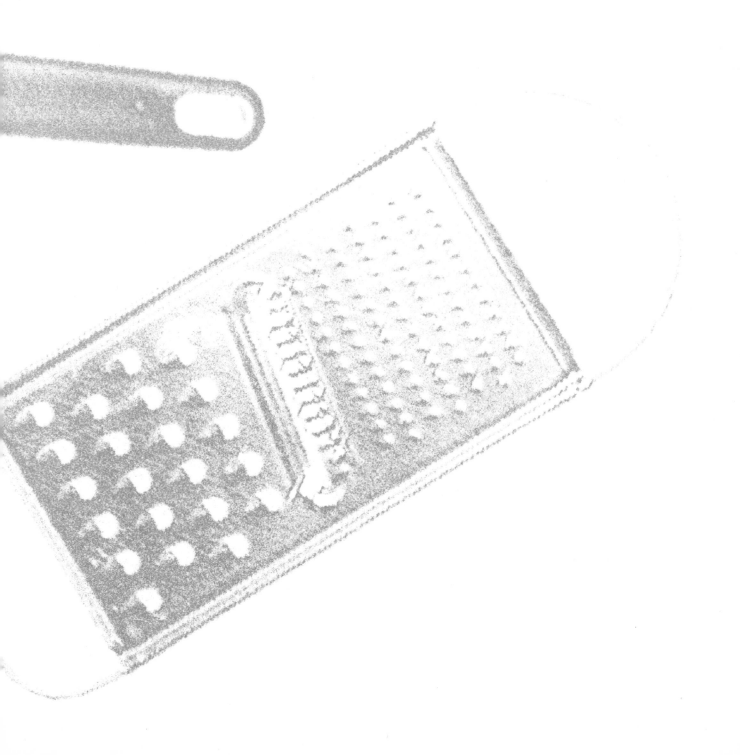

ENTERTAINING IS
A SELF-INFLICTED
WOUND

Even for professional cooks, entertaining can sometimes be a self-inflicted wound. When you have to invite the boss over for dinner, feed unwanted in-laws, or suffer drop-in guests who catch you when you're just too preoccupied to blurt out anything but "Stay for

supper?" it's hard to remain chipper, much less hospitable. For me the challenge of concealing dread dominates at least two or three occasions during the year. My suggestion for overcoming resistance to no-excuse entertaining is to plan a meal that looks like it took the better part of the month to prepare, but in reality only keeps you in the kitchen (preferably with an open bottle of wine) for just as much time as your guests are in the living and dining rooms (or outdoors in summer), while your spouse or cohost entertains and smiles.

Foods like marinated cuts of meat and homemade condiments are perfect for such

MENU

*Marinated
Pork Tenderloin*

*Sweet Potato
and Scallion Fritters*

*Baked Whole
Cauliflower*

Homemade Applesauce

*Pumpkin Pie with
Fresh Whipped Cream*

deceptions. They make it look as if you have really exhausted yourself, when all you have actually done is bought yourself some free time—time to pour yourself another glass of wine or make a couple of phone calls.

Admittedly the fritters will demand some of your attention, but they will also justify your continued presence in the kitchen. A word of caution though: Meals planned so deviously will mean at least two or more check-up visits from a disgruntled partner trying to find out what's keeping you in the kitchen. Once you have proven yourself by serving an impressive meal like this one, however, it really won't matter that you have spent the better part of the evening alone. ◼

....
Mustard is always good with pork, and it eliminates the need for sauces.

MARINATED PORK TENDERLOIN
....

I'm now told that pork is supposed to be a little pink inside, unlike in the old days when this was a sign of worms and instant death. If it's still bleeding, keep cooking.

  1 cup orange juice
  2 tablespoons soy sauce
  2 tablespoons fresh rosemary leaves,
    or 1 teaspoon dried
  4 garlic cloves, crushed
  1 1¹/₂-pound pork tenderloin
  Salt and pepper

In a small bowl whisk together the orange juice and soy sauce until well blended. Add the rosemary and garlic. Place the tenderloin lengthwise in a nonreactive baking dish. Pour the marinade over the meat. Cover with plastic wrap and chill for at least 2 hours. Brush or turn the meat occasionally to coat well.

Drain the meat and discard any excess marinade. Set the tenderloin on the broiler pan and lightly season with salt and pepper to taste. Grill about 3 inches from the heat for about 5 minutes on each side, or until the tenderloin is crisp on the outside and pink on the inside.

Let stand for about 5 minutes before serving. Serve sliced with good grainy mustard.

Serves 4

SWEET POTATO AND SCALLION FRITTERS

These fritters are best if cooked using a lighter oil like safflower or canola oil. Oils labeled "lite" are sometimes so light they are practically water-soluble. Use a natural oil instead.

4 eggs
4 medium sweet potatoes, peeled
6 scallions, green part only, cut lengthwise into thin strips
1 tablespoon minced fresh ginger
$^1/_2$ teaspoon nutmeg
$^1/_8$ teaspoon cayenne pepper
Tabasco sauce to taste
3 tablespoons all-purpose flour
Vegetable oil for frying

In a large bowl, beat the eggs.

Using a food processor, julienne the potatoes into thin strips. Add the potatoes to the bowl with the eggs. Stir in the scallion strips, ginger, nutmeg, cayenne, and Tabasco. Mix well, then add the flour a tablespoon at a time.

In a deep skillet, add $^1/_2$ inch of oil. Heat the oil slowly over medium-high heat until hot but not smoking. Drop forkfuls of potato mixture into the hot oil and cook until crispy, turning just once. Reduce the heat if fritters begin to burn or cook too quickly.

Drain the cooked fritters on a paper towel and keep warm in the oven on a low temperature setting until ready to serve. Repeat these steps until you have used all of the potato mixture, adding more oil to the skillet if needed.

Serves 6

BAKED WHOLE CAULIFLOWER

The first time I was served cauliflower whole it was steamed and seasoned with just a bit of table salt and finely ground pepper. It was beautiful but entirely too healthy for me. I thought it had a lot of potential, though, so I added a few ingredients to make it more appealing for those who only diet as a hobby.

1 head cauliflower
$^1/_2$ cup dry white wine
$^1/_2$ cup heavy cream
3 tablespoons unsalted butter
1 tablespoon fresh thyme leaves
$^1/_4$ teaspoon white pepper

Preheat the oven to 375° F.

Remove the cauliflower's outer leaves and some of the stem, but keep the head intact. With a sharp knife make an X about a $^1/_2$-inch deep in the remaining stem. Steam the cauliflower for about 15 minutes, or until tender when pierced with a fork. Carefully place the cauliflower in a buttered ovenproof dish.

In a saucepan over medium heat blend well the wine, heavy cream, butter, thyme, and pepper; don't let it reach a full boil. Pour the cream mixture over the cauliflower and bake for 10 to 15 minutes, or until the top has browned. Remove the cauliflower to a serving dish, taking care not to lose any florets, and pour the remaining sauce over the cauliflower. Serve immediately.

Serves 4

*Fresh fruit, **above**,
is an appetizing transi-
tion from dinner to the
inevitable . . . dessert.
With vegetables in dis-
guise, **right**, a meal
can be special served on
everyday plates.*

HOMEMADE APPLESAUCE

··

Making your own fresh applesauce will probably take only five minutes more than opening a jar of brand name. This is certainly worth the time.

2 pounds tart apples, such as McIntosh or
   Granny Smith
²/₃ cup water
¹/₂ teaspoon cinnamon
¹/₂ cup sugar
¹/₂ teaspoon lemon juice

Peel and slice the apples.

In a large saucepan, bring the water to a boil and add the apple slices. Cook the apples in the simmering water just until they are soft when pierced with a fork. Drain, then place into a food processor or blender with the cinnamon, sugar, and lemon juice. Puree to the desired consistency.

Remove the sauce to a bowl and chill, covered, until ready to serve.

Makes about 2 cups

PUMPKIN PIE WITH FRESH WHIPPED CREAM

··

I'm sure this pie belongs in the Thanksgiving menu, but you can make it quickly, which makes it perfect for this no-fault dinner, too.

3 eggs
1 29-ounce can solid pack pumpkin
1 cup sugar
2 teaspoons cinnamon
¹/₂ teaspoon ground nutmeg
¹/₂ teaspoon ground ginger
¹/₂ teaspoon ground cloves
1 cup light cream or whole milk
Pinch of salt

¹/₂ recipe A Very Basic Pie Crust (page 25)
Whipped Cream (recipe follows)

·····················

Like good peanut butter, "your own" homemade apple-sauce can be smooth to extra chunky.

Preheat the oven to 375° F.

Butter and flour a 9-inch pie plate.

In a large mixing bowl, lightly beat the eggs. Stir in the pumpkin, sugar, cinnamon, nutmeg, ginger, cloves, cream, and salt. Blend well.

Roll out the pastry dough into a circle large enough to cover the pie plate with about an inch extra all around. Fit the pastry dough into the pie plate, turn the edges under and pinch then pierce all over with a fork. Pour the pumpkin mixture slowly into the prepared pie shell. Place the pie on the middle rack of the oven and bake for 1 hour, or until the center is firm. If the edges begin to burn while the pie is baking, cover them with aluminum foil. Let cool and serve with whipped cream.

Makes 1 pie

WHIPPED CREAM

If you like whipped cream, you're probably already familiar with the aerosol can. Homemade whipped cream not only tastes better, it looks a lot more natural with food.

1 pint heavy cream

Place both a large metal bowl and a metal whisk in the freezer for about 20 to 30 minutes. Take the bowl out of the freezer and pour the cream in the bowl. Whisk the cream into stiff peaks. This might take a few minutes, but it produces the best fresh whipped cream and the most impressive forearms as well.

Makes about 2 cups

Now widely available all year, canned pumpkin lets you have pumpkin pie on more occasions than just Thanksgiving.

THE PATSY CLINE MEMORIAL CHILI DINNER

I have never personally sponsored a theme party myself, but they were very popular when I was in college—toga parties, "I Love Lucy" parties, and so on. There was one particularly elaborate theme, "Berlin in the 1950s," for which my roommate at the time re-created

the Berlin Wall using alternating bricks of cheddar and Jarlsberg cheese. It was cleverly executed—complete with graffiti and tiny bullet scars—and is one of my earliest food-styling memories. Until then I had been a virtual poster child of bad cuisine.

The closest I have ever come to a theme was a chili dinner I served to a large group of friends one bitter cold Sunday afternoon in December. Per-haps it was the country influence of the chili and corn bread or the mass quantities of southwestern beer we consumed at breakneck speed, but after a very short time, dinner had become a Patsy Cline music marathon.

Patsy Cline, the greatest of many great country music stars, went down in flames in a plane crash in 1963, leaving us, her fans, with great tunes and a semisuccessful movie bio starring

MENU

Patsy Cline Memorial Chili

Scallion and Gorgonzola Corn Bread

Green Salad

Apple and Pine Nut Pie

Jessica Lange. Maybe it was the beer, maybe it was the music—but by dessert we had all decided to name my new chili recipe after Patsy. The Madonna of country music deserves something more to remember her by than just a four-record set offered only on late-night TV. ∎

PATSY CLINE MEMORIAL CHILI

Chili, like spaghetti sauce, is best left up to individual interpretation. This is the basic Patsy Cline Memorial recipe, from which I deviate every time I make chili. Served with a simple green salad, this is a well-balanced meal.

1 pound chorizo sausage
1 tablespoon minced garlic
$1/2$ cup coarsely chopped celery
1 large yellow onion, coarsely chopped
1 large red bell pepper, seeds removed, then diced
2 jalapeño peppers, finely minced
1 28-ounce can crushed tomatoes
1 6-ounce can tomato paste
1 $14^1/2$-ounce can chicken stock
1 teaspoon ground cumin
1 teaspoon dried sage
$1/2$–1 teaspoon cayenne pepper
1 teaspoon red pepper flakes
3 tablespoons chili powder
1 $15^1/2$-ounce can dark red kidney beans, drained and rinsed well
1 pound cooked medium shrimp (see Note)

In a large stockpot, sauté the sausage over a medium heat until browned. Drain on a paper towel and set aside.

Remove all but 1 tablespoon of the remaining fat from the stockpot. Stir in the garlic and sauté until golden. Add the celery, onion, bell pepper, and jalapeño, and sauté until the onion is browned and the celery is wilted. Stir in the crushed tomatoes, tomato paste, and chicken stock. Simmer over a low to medium heat, stirring often until thickened and well blended, about 25 to 30 minutes.

Cut the sausage into $1/2$-inch pieces and add them to the sauce. Stir in the cumin, sage, cayenne, red pepper flakes, and chili powder and simmer for another 30 minutes. Fold in the beans and shrimp and heat through. Keep warm over low heat until ready to serve.

Serves 8 to 10

Note: Cooked shrimp is available in the fresh seafood section of the supermarket.

SCALLION AND GORGONZOLA CORN BREAD

The simple addition of Gorgonzola and chopped scallion make this otherwise routine corn bread something rather impressive. It is served right from the baking dish, cut into wedges.

$1^1/4$ cups yellow cornmeal
$3/4$ cup all-purpose flour
4 teaspoons baking powder
1 teaspoon sugar
$1/2$ teaspoon salt
1 cup milk
1 egg, lightly beaten
1 tablespoon unsalted butter
$3/4$ cup crumbled Gorgonzola
$1/2$ cup chopped scallion, green and white parts

Preheat the oven to 400° F. Put a 9-inch ovenproof skillet in the oven while preheating.

Sift together the cornmeal, flour, baking powder, sugar, and salt in a large bowl. Quickly mix in the milk and egg to make a coarse batter.

Take the heated skillet out of the oven, put the butter into it, and brush it around all sides as it melts. Pour $1/2$ to $3/4$ of the batter into the prepared skillet. Add the crumbled cheese. Pour the remaining batter over the cheese, then top with the scallion.

Bake for 25 minutes, or until the top is golden and the center is firm to the touch. Let stand for 5 to 10 minutes, then run a knife around the edge. Cut into wedges and serve.

Makes 10 to 12 wedges

A VERY BASIC PIE CRUST

This recipe should take all the mystery out of perfecting the "perfect" pie crust. The dough can be made ahead of time and stored in the freezer for up to two weeks. If you still don't have a food processor, use the old-fashioned pastry blender.

1$1/2$ cups all-purpose flour, measured by dipping the measuring cup into the flour then leveling it off with a knife
$1/2$ teaspoon salt
$1/2$ cup (1 stick) unsalted butter, ice cold, cut up into $1/2$-inch cubes
3–4 tablespoons ice water

In a food processor combine the flour and salt. Pulse once and stop the machine. Gradually add the butter in two or three steps, pulsing only a few times after each addition. Add the water tablespoon by tablespoon, pulsing after each addition until the dough looks crumbly in the work bowl. Try to use only 3 tablespoons of water. Remove the blade and form the dough into a ball. Flatten the dough and chill between two sheets of wax paper for at least an hour.

Makes enough pastry for two 9-inch crusts or one 9-inch 2-crust pie

APPLE AND PINE NUT PIE

It took a couple of trips to the American Southwest for me to realize that piñolas, or pine nuts, weren't just for savory dishes. When they are used fresh, their texture is more profound than their flavor, so they complement sweets and desserts. Pine nuts are most affordable squeezed out of a pinecone, or alternatively from the health food store or produce market, rather than from the spice department at the grocery store.

8 Granny Smith apples, peeled, cored, and thinly sliced
1 cup milk
$1/2$ recipe A Very Basic Pie Crust (see this page)
1 egg yolk, lightly beaten
$1/4$ cup lightly packed light brown sugar
1 teaspoon each cinnamon and nutmeg
$1/4$ cup ($1/2$ stick) unsalted butter, cut into $1/2$-inch pieces
$1/3$ cup pine nuts

Place the sliced apples in a large bowl, and pour in the milk. Let the mixture stand while you prepare the pie crust.

Preheat the oven to 400° F.

Butter and flour a 9-inch pie plate. Roll out the pastry dough to $1/4$-inch thick on a well-floured surface. Fit the pastry into the prepared pie plate and pierce the bottom with a fork.

Drain the milk from the apples and discard. Add the egg yolk, sugar, cinnamon, and nutmeg to the apples and stir to coat. Pour the apple mixture into the pie crust and top with the butter and the pine nuts.

Bake on the middle rack of the oven for 30 to 35 minutes, or until the filling is bubbly and the pine nuts are toasted. If the crust's edges brown too much, cover the top with aluminum foil. Let stand for at least 20 minutes, or let cool completely to room temperature, before serving.

Makes one 9-inch pie

DINNER AT
ROSEMARY'S

One thing I like a lot better than entertaining in my own home is going over to someone

else's house and watching them do most of the work. Not that it's the basis of our friend-

ship, but my friend Rosemary does this well and often. Rosemary has studied under some

pretty impressive chefs in Italy and both
her mother and father have spent lots of

MENU

Rosemary's Risotto

Broccoli di Rape

Sausage

*Frozen Yogurt
and Fresh Berries*

time in the kitchen, so she knows what she
is doing. Dinner at Rosemary's sometimes
can take hours if not all day. It's a great family occasion with lots of arguing and laughter. The conversation always centers around
exotic foods, good wine, and the family hob-

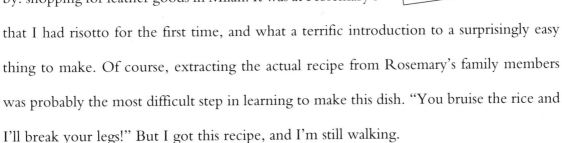

by: shopping for leather goods in Milan. It was at Rosemary's

that I had risotto for the first time, and what a terrific introduction to a surprisingly easy

thing to make. Of course, extracting the actual recipe from Rosemary's family members

was probably the most difficult step in learning to make this dish. "You bruise the rice and

I'll break your legs!" But I got this recipe, and I'm still walking.

Rosemary still goes back to her old neighborhood in Brooklyn to do some of her food shopping. She usually brings me a souvenir—a lesser-known herb, beautiful fresh grape leaves, dried peppers, or chains of dried okra (which can be troublesome to cook but with a little tempera paint make great costume jewelry). This is where she swears you can find the best sausage and produce, namely the broccoli di rape, available in Brooklyn at almost anytime of the year. Needless to say her pantry is the closest thing America has to a food museum. ◼

Broccoli di Rape is full of all those trendy nutrients we keep hearing about . . . and maybe even some we haven't.

ROSEMARY'S RISOTTO

This main course rice dish requires just a few ingredients and a few minutes of careful stirring. Nothing more. Don't try to substitute long grain rice, though. It may taste okay, but it won't be risotto.

1 bunch (about 15 stalks) thin asparagus
3 tablespoons extra virgin olive oil
1 large red onion, diced
1¹/₂ cups raw arborio (short grain Italian) rice
1 46-ounce can chicken stock
1 tablespoon unsalted butter
4 tablespoons grated Parmesan cheese
Salt and pepper

Rinse the asparagus. Trim off any tough ends and cut into 1¹/₂-inch pieces.

In a large saucepan or stockpot, heat the oil and sauté the onion and asparagus for about 4 minutes. Add the uncooked rice to the asparagus and onion and sauté for another 2 minutes. Lower the heat and add ¹/₂ cup of stock to the rice. Stir gently and cover.

Continue to add stock to the rice as it is absorbed. Continue until all of the stock is used, stirring gently and just often enough to keep the rice from getting soggy. Cooking time is about 25 minutes. The rice should be a little crunchy. Fold in the butter and the cheese, salt and pepper to taste, and serve immediately.

Serves 4

BROCCOLI DI RAPE

You don't have to go all the way back to the old neighborhood for broccoli di rape (a vitamin-packed substitute for broccoli or spinach). It's available at most specialty produce shops or supermarkets.

4 pounds (2 bunches) broccoli di rape
6 tablespoons extra virgin olive oil, plus
   additional oil for serving
2 garlic cloves
Salt and pepper

Remove any brown leaves from the broccoli di rape and discard. Trim the vegetables so the stems are uniform in size (about 3 or 4 inches long); this is important so that the stalks and florets cook evenly. Soak the broccoli di rape in a pot of cold water to rinse away sand.

In a large saucepan, heat the oil over a medium heat. Cut the garlic cloves in half, add them to the oil and sauté until golden. Lower the heat. Shake the broccoli di rape stalks and florets of most of the excess water and add to the oil. Add salt and pepper to taste. Cook, covered, 3 to 4 minutes, stirring occasionally to ensure even cooking. Remove the pan from the heat and let stand, covered, for another 2 minutes to finish cooking.

Broccoli di rape should remain dark green. If it turns pale that means it's overcooked. (Sorry!) Before serving, add a little olive oil and toss to coat.

Serves 4

No need to prepare every course yourself when frozen yogurt is around the corner.

SAUSAGE

Rosemary says that the best sausage is thin and is sold in coils. It's sometimes called luganega and is available in most supermarkets or Italian butcher shops.

3 tablespoons water
1–1½ pounds sweet or hot Italian pork
   sausage, in a coil or links

Put the water into a large skillet and turn the heat to medium high. When the water begins to steam, add the sausage, prick it with a fork, and cover. Bring to a boil for a few minutes, then lower the heat. Turn and flip the sausage and continue cooking, uncovered, until the water has boiled away and the sausage is crisp and brown. Serve immediately.

Serves 4

A COCKTAIL PARTY
OF ONE'S OWN

As I prepare for my very own cocktail party, I ponder exactly how many of these soirées I've actually attended. How many times have I agreed to suggestions I never even heard, due to the host's numbing his guests auditory senses with really loud music until they perfected their

lip-reading skills. How many times have I been offered saucissons en croute, which are just "pigs in a blanket" to me?

Hosting a cocktail party can be one of entertaining's greatest challenges. It is nevertheless a rite of passage: you can't be a responsible grown-up until you have dispensed a few gallons of clam dip. It's also the best way to return a bunch of invitations all at once. Come to think of it, this might be fun.

As I inspect this evening's surplus of store-bought ice, most of which inevitably melts in the bathtub simply because no freezer is large enough to store a future watershed, I promise myself to remain calm. I've been to my fill of parties

MENU

Apricot and Watercress Sandwiches

Cucumber and Salmon Sandwiches

Julie Pemberton's Tapenade

Skewered Scallops with Bacon

Camembert in Herbed Pastry

The Proper Bar

where the host wanders nervously from guest to guest whispering, "Do you think everyone is having a good time?" My guests, too, are professionals, and know well enough how to move on and refresh their drinks if an awkward conversational silence becomes too loud. I also know that cocktail parties (especially one's own) are not the occasion for pairing hopelessly mismatched friends in hopes of consummating a marriage before evening's end.

Just as I position my Camembert, the doorbell rings. I'm gratified to know that at least one person I know isn't too proud to be casually on time. ■

....
Take a cookie cutter to the Cucumber and Salmon Sandwiches.

APRICOT AND WATERCRESS SANDWICHES
....

Like Freud, I believe that it is impossible to be bored if you have something in your mouth. That's why hors d'oeuvres and finger foods are crucial elements of a successful cocktail party. When guests aren't devouring these delicious sandwiches, they can talk to each other about what's in them.

1/4 cup dried apricots
8 ounces cream cheese
1 loaf thinly sliced dark or pumpernickel bread
1 bunch watercress, rinsed, trimmed, and any tough stems removed
Salt and pepper

In a food processor, combine the apricots and cream cheese and puree until smooth.

Liberally spread one side of each slice of bread with the cream cheese mixture. Top half of the slices with sprigs of watercress, season to taste with salt and pepper, then top with the remaining slices of bread, cream cheese side down. Using a knife or cookie cutter, cut into small sandwiches.

Makes about 20 sandwiches

Crackers and cheese
may be a cliché,
but like most
clichés, it's an idea
that bears repeating.
Dress the platter
with fresh herbs.

CUCUMBER AND SALMON SANDWICHES

This is the sort of thing the English serve at tea, but it's just fine with something stronger.

8 ounces cream cheese
$^1/_3$ pound sliced smoked salmon
1 loaf thinly sliced white bread
$^1/_2$ cucumber, very thinly sliced

In a food processor, combine the cream cheese and the smoked salmon and puree until smooth.

Spread one side of each slice of bread with the cream cheese mixture. Top half of the slices with the cucumbers, then top with the remaining slices of bread, cream cheese side down. Using a knife or cookie cutter, cut into small sandwiches.

Makes about 20 sandwiches

My taste in hors
d'oeuvres sometimes
runs from the sub-
lime, **right**, to the
ridiculous, **above**,
but the conversation
never dies.

JULIE PEMBERTON'S TAPENADE

I once asked my colleague Julie what she would serve if her apartment wasn't so small and she was actually able to accommodate guests.

"Tapenade," she replied. I thought this was a great idea not only because it requires so little work, but also because it doesn't take up much space.

Serve the tapenade on endive leaves with a soft ripe cheese or on toast points.

1 cup pitted Niçoise olives (see Note)
3 anchovy fillets
3–4 garlic cloves
Juice of 1 lemon
2 teaspoons capers
$1/4$–$1/2$ cup olive oil

In a food processor combine the olives, anchovies, garlic, lemon juice, and capers.

With the machine running slowly, gradually add up to but no more than $1/2$ cup of oil, just enough to make the mixture spreadable. Allow the machine to run until the mixture is smooth, about a minute longer.

Makes 1 cup

Note: You can get the olives at the supermarket deli section or at a gourmet store. Remove the pits yourself, with knife, fingernails, and patience.

Anything served with lots of grapes on endive has to look good. Use this idea to death.

When the cocktail cannon sounds, these rations are as valuable as canned milk during wartime.

SKEWERED SCALLOPS WITH BACON

Some cocktail parties seem designed for vegetarians, with crudités on every tray. This recipe is a reward for the patient nonvegetarian party-goer, and it's easily half the work of whittling a mountain of radish roses.

15 strips lean bacon, cut in half vertically
1 pound (about 30) sea scallops, rinsed well
    and patted dry
Juice of 2 limes
$1/2$ teaspoon dried red pepper flakes
    (or to taste)

Immerse 30 wooden skewers in warm water for about 10 or 15 minutes. This will make it easier for guests to remove the scallops from them.

Carefully wrap a strip of bacon around a scallop, then secure it with a skewer. Repeat until all the scallops and bacon are used.

Place the prepared skewers in a medium bowl and pour the lime juice over them. Let stand, loosely covered, for about an hour. Arrange the skewers on a broiler tray and sprinkle with the red pepper flakes. Broil for about 5 minutes on each side, or until the scallops are cooked through and the bacon is crispy. Serve on the skewers.

Makes 30 skewers

CAMEMBERT IN HERBED PASTRY

This is my deviation from the timeless brie en croute—a virtual party staple and as practical as ice.

1 $17^1/4$-ounce package frozen puff pastry
    sheets
$1/4$ cup chopped fresh basil or Italian parsley
4 garlic cloves, finely chopped
2 $8^1/2$-ounce Camembert rounds
1 egg white

Thaw the pastry according to the package instructions. Preheat the oven to 350° F.

Roll out each pastry sheet on a well-floured surface. Spread the chopped basil or parsley evenly over both pastry sheets, and sprinkle with the garlic. Place a round of cheese in the center of each pastry sheet and wrap the pastry around the cheese. Twist the top to seal and cut away any excess pastry. Brush the pastry with the egg white to seal all the edges.

Place both rounds on an ungreased cookie sheet and bake for 20 to 25 minutes, or until the pastry is golden. Serve with crackers and honey mustard or capers.

Serves 10 to 20

SUBURBAN PICNIC
FOR THE SLAVES OF NEW YORK

MENU

*Raw Cherrystone
Clams with Dad's Red
Seafood Sauce*

Barbecued Chicken

Sweet Potato Chips

*Knockwurst
and Tomato Salad*

Grilled Corn on the Cob

Blueberry Pie

Much to the displeasure of my city-dwelling friends, I very proudly live in the suburbs. To some my environment is a curse; to others, a phenomenon. Urbanites usually consider my choice of address proof that I am culturally starved, or just going through a "Green Acres" phase, simply because I don't live within walking distance of a cappuccino bar or a mugging. These are the same friends who refer to small cities like Yonkers or Bronxville as "the country."

Throughout most of the year I listen patiently to all the many reasons why I should drop everything, drain my birdbath, and move back to the city. Of course none of this matters once summer comes, the elements prevail, and Manhattan becomes a meteorologist's nightmare. Suddenly the once-forbidden and maligned suburbs become an oasis for the urban-weary. No one with a backyard, a grill, or a lawn jockey is safe.

Every summer, generally starting in early July and persisting through Labor Day, all of my incoming phone calls begin the same way. "Is this the hottest summer or what?" Needless to say these conversations usually lead to the same destination. "Wouldn't it be nice if we came up there sometime?" When I reach the end of my repertoire of excuses—"I was really planning to clean the cat box that day"—I figure the best way to satisfy them is with picnic food typical enough so they know they're out of the concrete jungle, but not so corny that they think I don't have indoor plumbing or cable. ∎

DAD'S RED SEAFOOD SAUCE

For some of us, Dad's sauce has made raw seafood and shellfish palatable. It is also great with boiled shrimp, lobster, or crab.

1 cup ketchup
1/2 cup chili sauce (see Note)
1 tablespoon lemon juice
1 teaspoon prepared horseradish, or to taste
Dash of Tabasco sauce

In a bowl mix together all ingredients until well blended. Serve by the spoonful over raw cherrystone or littleneck clams.

Makes 1 1/2 to 2 cups

Note: Dad uses Heinz's Chili Sauce straight from the bottle.

Though it flies in the face of today's Fear of Fat cuisine, I like messy food at a picnic, like Barbecued Chicken and Sweet Potato Chips, above, and opposite.

BARBECUED CHICKEN

The marinade for this chicken is also tasty as a bar-becue sauce on any loose vegetables you might have around—eggplant, zucchini, summer squash, onions, and so on. Sliced thin, liberally brushed with marinade, and grilled alongside the chicken, they can serve as the mandatory vegetable side dish. For the chicken, I generally buy breast quarters and leave the breast on the bone. It's usually a bit more affordable than the boneless breasts and the bone provides a handle. If you don't like your chicken blackened, just skip the marinating step and brush the sauce on both sides of the chicken during the last 10 minutes of grilling.

  1 cup lemon juice
  3/4 cup honey
  1/2 teaspoon red pepper flakes
  1 bunch chives, chopped
  3 pounds chicken breasts, quartered

In a small bowl, whisk together the lemon juice and honey until well blended. Stir in the red pepper flakes and chives.

Place all of the chicken in a bowl. Pour the marinade over the chicken and toss to coat. Cover and refrigerate for at least one hour.

Start the fire while the chicken is marinating.

Grill the chicken over hot coals. (Do not pour any leftover marinade over the cooked chicken. Throw it away.)

Serves 4 to 6

SWEET POTATO CHIPS

Yes, these are messy and time-consuming to make, but they are greatly appreciated by those who are used to chips that come in a bag. If you make a large batch once a year you'll not only be confining a mess but possibly starting a tradition.

  4–5 large sweet potatoes
  Juice of 1/2 lemon
  Canola oil for deep frying
  2 dried chili peppers
  Salt

Using a mandolin, a slicing machine, or even a knife and your own steady hand, slice the potatoes as thinly as possible.

Place the slices in a large bowl filled with cold water into which you have squeezed the lemon juice.

With the cover nearby, heat about 1 1/2 inches of the oil in a large pot and toss in the chili peppers. The oil is hot enough when it has reached 350° F. on a thermometer or when water (just a drop!) sizzles when splattered on top.

Blot the chips dry on a clean paper towel and drop one by one into the oil. Fry the chips until the centers are crisp, about 5 to 7 minutes. If necessary, add more oil. Drain the chips well on paper towels. Salt to taste.

Serves 6

*The perfect beginning
(Clams with Dad's
Red Seafood Sauce),*
above, *deserves the
perfect ending
(Blueberry Pie),*
right.

KNOCKWURST AND TOMATO SALAD

The Swiss sometimes refer to knockwurst as cervelats, if that makes you feel any better, or think of it as an upscale answer to hot dogs.

4 tablespoons good olive oil
3 teaspoons balsamic vinegar
1 tablespoon grainy mustard
1/4 cup chopped fresh basil
1/2 pound knockwurst, skin or casing removed, sliced into 1/4-inch pieces
5 ripe beefsteak tomatoes, rinsed, stemmed, and cut into 1/2-inch wedges

In a large bowl, whisk together the oil, vinegar, and mustard until well blended. Stir in the basil. Add the knockwurst and tomatoes and toss to coat.

Serves 4 to 6

GRILLED CORN ON THE COB

In my opinion, the best corn is the bicolor type often called butter and sugar. In the northeast it is most widely available—and freshest—during July, August, and early September.

If I'm cooking corn for myself I eat it steamed with no butter, salt, or seasonings. The recipe here is probably more practical for a large group of people, as it comes to the table already seasoned and ready to eat.

8 ears corn, husks left on
1/2 cup (1 stick) unsalted butter
3 tablespoons chopped fresh basil or parsley, or 1 1/2 teaspoons dried
Juice of 1 lemon
Salt and pepper

Not your typical weenies and beans . . . but as close as a salad can get.

Fill a large pot with water and soak the corn for an hour.

In a small saucepan over low heat melt the butter and stir in the basil and lemon juice. Add salt and pepper to taste.

Carefully pull the husks away from the corn, but don't pull them off. Remove all the silk, brush each ear with the butter mixture and pull the husks back into place. Secure each ear with a loop of kitchen string. Grill the corn for about 20 to 25 minutes, turning often. Serve in the husk.

Serves 4 to 6

BLUEBERRY PIE

If you are daunted by the very notion of "Baking," just remember that a homemade pie with oozing syrup and irregular crust is far more appealing than the perfectly formed and lifeless bakery version. Do the pie crust ahead so the pressure is not so great.

1 A Very Simple Pie Crust (page 25)
5 cups fresh blueberries, rinsed well and any stems removed
1 tablespoon lemon juice
1 teaspoon vanilla extract
$1/2$ cup sugar
5 tablespoons unsalted butter, ice cold and cut into $1/4$-inch pieces

Preheat the oven to 400° F.

Roll half of the dough into a large circle on a well-floured surface. If this is your first pie, keep lifting the edges and dusting more flour underneath as you roll. Fit the dough into an 8-inch pie plate and pierce all over with a fork.

In a large bowl, add the blueberries, lemon juice, vanilla, and sugar, and mix well. Pour the blueberry mixture into the prepared pie crust. Top with the butter.

Roll the remaining pie dough into a large circle. Place over the pie, fold and crimp the edges. (Pressing them with a fork is fine.) Cut holes in the top for ventilation.

Bake for 30 to 40 minutes or until the top is golden and filling is bubbly.

Serves 6 to 8

JUSTIFY MY LUNCH

Lunch once meant something that was brought to school everyday in a brown paper bag: bologna on white topped with blinding yellow mustard, the much-dreaded egg salad, or, if I was lucky, PB&J, something even the most sophisticated palate can still unabashedly

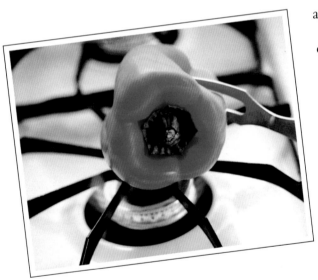

appreciate. (To me, this and a tall glass of chocolate milk are the highpoints of American Cuisine.) Followed by a Twinkie, a Scooter Pie, or a piece of fruit that generally went back and forth from school six times before Mom tossed it out, lunch was routine but reasonably nutritious.

MENU

*Roast Pepper
and Gorgonzola
Sandwiches*

Homemade Cole Slaw

Orange Spice Tea

Today, my lunch is something "take-out," generally unhealthy, or allegedly fat-and-cholesterol-free, chased by what's left of the double espresso that didn't spill out into the bag in transport. Then, up until very recently, there was a workingman's dessert: as many cigarettes as I could smoke in the remaining minutes of an all-too-short lunch hour. Hard as I try to "make over"—a term used all too casually for what is in reality a profound

struggle—the lunches I grab during the week are by and large mostly unnatural. This makes no sense, especially when my third largest monthly expense is a health club membership, but it does make the weekends worth looking forward to: on Saturday I prepare a quick, tasty, and relatively wholesome sandwich and enjoy it for more than sixty minutes. ◾

ROAST PEPPER AND GORGONZOLA SANDWICHES

I could write a book entirely about Gorgonzola, the blue cheese of the Italians. Used in moderation, it doesn't enhance your breath as much as its cousins —Roquefort, Danish blue, or Limburger—seem to do, but it packs just as much kick.

3–4 large bell peppers, preferably yellow, red, and green
1/4 cup extra virgin olive oil
1 garlic clove, finely minced
1 teaspoon crushed fresh rosemary leaves, or 1/2 teaspoon dried
1/4 teaspoon coarsely ground black pepper
6–8 slices toasted semolina bread
1/3 cup crumbled Gorgonzola

Leave peppers whole and rinse well under cold running water.

If you're using a gas stove, place a pepper on the end of a long-handled fork or a skewer and hold directly above the flame, cooking until the pepper is black and charred all over. Repeat with remaining peppers. If you're using an electric stove, place a few peppers at a time under the broiler, turning every few minutes until charred all over.

Remove the peppers from the heat and place in a brown paper bag. Seal the bag and let stand until the peppers have cooled, about 20 minutes.

Remove the peppers from the bag, and peel them. (The skin should separate easily from the pepper.) Cut away the stem, then core, seed, and quarter them (see Note).

In a small bowl, combine the oil, garlic, and rosemary. Lay the roasted pepper quarters flat in a pie plate or dish, pour the oil over them, and sprinkle with pepper. Let stand about an hour.

Divide the peppers evenly among half of the bread slices. Top with the crumbled cheese and the remaining slices of bread.

Makes 3 to 4 sandwiches

Note: If you want to keep a few roasted peppers for later, store them covered in olive oil in a tightly sealed container at room temperature until ready to use.

If time allows, you might want to do something really strenuous, like set the table.

Olive oils are great infused with dried herbs and used for salads and marinades—an impressive staple.

HOMEMADE COLE SLAW

This dish is best when left in the refrigerator overnight.

1 pound (about $1/2$ head) green cabbage
$1/2$ pound (about $1/4$ head) red cabbage
4 large carrots, peeled and coarsely chopped
Juice of 1 lemon
1 cup mayonnaise
$1/4$ cup milk
1 tablespoon balsamic vinegar
2 tablespoons grainy mustard
$1/2$ teaspoon dried tarragon
Salt and pepper

Remove, wash, and reserve the best looking outer leaves from both heads of cabbage. Wrap them in a damp paper towel and store in the refrigerator for later use.

Shred the cabbages into a large bowl. Stir in the chopped carrots. Pour in the lemon juice and toss to coat. In a separate bowl, mix together the mayonnaise, milk, vinegar, mustard, and tarragon. Pour the dressing over the cabbage mixture and toss well. Season with salt and pepper to taste and chill for at least 2 hours. To serve, line a serving bowl with the reserved cabbage leaves and arrange the cole slaw in the center.

Makes about 12 servings

ORANGE SPICE TEA

I drink iced tea all year long. This tea has a flavor that is suitable for all seasons.

3 teaspoons loose Orange Pekoe tea
1 pod star anise (see Note)
3 tablespoons sugar
2 oranges
6 cups water

In a large Mason or Ball jar place the tea, star anise, and the sugar. Cut one of the oranges into equal quarters and squeeze the juice into the jar, then add the peels. Bring the water to a rolling boil and pour into the jar. Let the tea stand for 10 minutes. Strain the tea into a pitcher and let cool to room temperature.

When ready to serve, slice the remaining orange and divide the slices evenly among the glasses. Serve in tall glasses with lots of ice.

Makes 6 cups

Note: Star anise is available in either the dried herb and spice or the ethnic foods section of your local supermarket.

....
Once you've got the peppers grilled, these very casually constructed sandwiches take no time at all.

THE OBLIGATORY PARENTAL DINNER

Once a year my parents, like many others, return from another winter in Florida. About an hour later the phone rings. "So when are we coming to dinner?" "I'm fine, and you?" I stall to ponder my schedule. But of course I surrender. I've used virtually every excuse known to man, and let's face it, they know where I live.

I hang up the phone and am suddenly overwhelmed by memories of sitting alone in a dimly lit dining room crying over uneaten spinach, hoping vainly to avoid choking back the once piping-hot greens. My mother always reminded us that there were starving babies in faraway countries who, if given the chance, would do just about anything for a bite of that spinach. On one occasion, I couldn't help but mention that if packaged correctly this very spinach could easily be sealed into business-size envelopes and mailed to the aforementioned tribes of hungry people. My mother never readily entertained such suggestions, and I was very often left to try to swallow my petrified side dishes before dawn the next day.

MENU

Marinated Roast
Game Hens with Assorted
Wild Mushrooms

Brussels Sprouts

Grilled Polenta

Mother's Apple Crisp

Of the many things my parents have in common, I now seem to recall that they share a dislike of carrots. Suddenly all I can think about are recipes with carrots, an entire meal of carrots—carrot soup, carrot soufflé, carrot bread, peas and carrots, carrot cake. This menu is theoretically possible, but it is to my credit that I don't express resentment of old wounds in the menu I plan for my parents. I even conclude the meal with Mother's Apple Crisp. To my mother's credit, she never reminds me of how much better she makes it herself. ■

MARINATED ROAST GAME HENS WITH ASSORTED WILD MUSHROOMS

Roast game hens are simple and an impressive departure from the all-too-familiar roast chicken, especially when served with an assortment of fresh wild mushrooms. These mushrooms are now widely available at most grocery stores and produce markets. To cut down on the expense, mix them with plain white or button mushrooms.

4 Rock Cornish game hens
$1/2$ cup olive oil
$1/4$ cup balsamic vinegar
2 tablespoons fresh thyme leaves, or $1 1/2$ teaspoons dried
Juice of 2 lemons
3 tablespoons honey
Salt and pepper
4 cups assorted wild mushrooms, such as shiitake, cremini, chanterelle, champignon, and so on

Inside the game hens are the birds' liver and gizzards. Remove them and throw them away. (You could save them for another use but you know you won't. Or try giving them to the cats.) Rinse the hens inside and out, then pat dry.

In a large bowl, whisk together the oil and vinegar until well blended. Add the thyme, lemon juice, honey, and salt and pepper to taste.

Place the hens in a large plastic bag, pour $3/4$ of the marinade over the hens, seal the bag, and put the bag in a bowl in case it drips. Refrigerate for at least 2 hours, turning the bag often.

Preheat the oven to 350° F. Remove the hens from the marinade, arrange on a rack in a roasting pan, and fill the pan with $1/2$ inch of cold water. Roast the hens for 30 to 35 minutes.

While the hens are roasting, rinse and trim any tough stems from the mushrooms. Larger mushrooms should be quartered or cut up into smaller pieces. Place the mushrooms in a large bowl and pour the remaining marinade over them. Toss to coat. Pour the mushrooms around the hens in the roasting pan and continue roasting for another 10 to 15 minutes.

Serves 4

BRUSSELS SPROUTS

It's popular to hate Brussels sprouts, and ever since President Bush let his dislike of broccoli be known, it has been proper to warn your host or hostess about your personal food blacklist. If your parents have not already banned Brussels sprouts, try this recipe for them. They will be impressed to see you eating something green, and at how good a vegetable can taste if it is cooked correctly.

3 cups Brussels sprouts, rinsed well, and
    trimmed of any discolored leaves
2 tablespoons unsalted butter
1/2 cup dry white wine
Salt and pepper

Either cut the Brussels sprouts in half length-wise or cut an X about a quarter of an inch deep in their stems. (This will ensure that both the inside and outside are equally cooked.)

In a medium saucepan, melt the butter over medium heat. Stir in the Brussels sprouts and toss to coat. Pour in the white wine and bring to a simmer. Lower the heat and cover the pan. Let simmer for 7 to 10 minutes or until the sprouts are tender but still firm. (Watch the heat carefully—the odor of scorched sprouts can ruin a meal.) Salt and pepper to taste. Serve immediately, preferably in a covered dish.

Serves 4

GRILLED POLENTA

I sometimes cook polenta (Italian cornmeal mush) with white wine instead of water or stock for a sweeter result.

2 tablespoons vegetable oil
1 medium onion, chopped
3 scallions, green and white parts, chopped
2 cups chicken or vegetable stock
2 cups water
1/2 teaspoon salt
1 1/4 cups yellow cornmeal
1/3 cup shredded cheddar cheese
2 tablespoons chopped fresh sage (or 1 tea-spoon dried)
2 tablespoons unsalted butter, melted

Butter an 8-inch pie plate or baking dish.

Heat the oil in a large heavy saucepan over medium heat. Stir in the onion and scallions and sauté until lightly browned. Stir in the stock, water, and salt, and bring to a simmer.

Slowly add the cornmeal in a thin stream, stirring constantly, until the mixture becomes smooth and thick, about 3 to 4 minutes. Remove from the heat and fold in the cheddar cheese and sage.

Spread the mixture in the prepared pie plate and allow it to cool to room temperature. It will solidify and pull away from the plate edges as it cools. Score the cooled polenta into equal slices.

Preheat the broiler. Brush the polenta with the melted butter and place under the broiler until the top is golden and crispy. Serve immediately.

Makes one 8-inch pie

MOTHER'S APPLE CRISP

This is one of the easiest desserts I know. Granny Smith apples are probably the best apples to use because of their firmness. Unlike McIntosh, or Red or Golden Delicious, they hold up under fire, even when sliced very thin.

8 Granny Smith apples, peeled, cored, and
    sliced
1/2 cup water
1 teaspoon cinnamon
1/4 teaspoon nutmeg
1 cup unsifted all-purpose flour
7 tablespoons unsalted butter
3/4 cup granulated sugar

Preheat the oven to 400° F.

Butter a 7 1/2 x 11 3/4-inch ovenproof baking dish and scatter the peeled apples evenly across the bottom. Pour in the water and sprinkle with the cinnamon and nutmeg.

In a small bowl, mix together the flour, butter, and sugar with a fork or pastry blender until crumbly. Spread this mixture evenly over the apples. Bake for 30 minutes or until the top is crispy and the apple filling is bubbly.

Serve with generous amounts of whipped cream, ice cream, or maple syrup.

Serves 6 to 8

A PRESEASON
BREAKFAST AT
THE BEACH

It had been a winter best measured by bad haircuts, perplexing financial and romantic entanglements, and just too much emotional backlash—an endless winter, gray, bleak, and with snow right through March. But finally the mercury had managed to struggle to a tolerable 60 degrees and the winter-weary made their spring debut at the local picnic ground.

With little notice some friends and I packed our late-model station wagon with what we thought, and still do believe, to be the proper beach picnic rations —homemade muffins, coffee, and mimosas—and headed for our favorite spot right next to the water. Judging from the surrounding picnics, we were clearly the best prepared. Sea gulls started up as we popped the first in what would become a succession of champagne bottles. Despite our own festive mood, we could not help but notice the envy on the faces of our neighboring picnickers as the aroma of fresh coffee and grilled muffins wafted past them from our grill. Clad in the most expensive cross-training outfits money can buy,

MENU

Grilled Banana Muffins

Grilled Orange Muffins

Grilled Sausages

Minted Melon Salad

Mimosas

Coffee

they were otherwise meagerly equipped with only the Sunday magazine section and a take-out cup. Perhaps we were more simply attired, but our picnic was clearly the envy of the park. "Too bad," was our response as we continued to enjoy our preseason breakfast at the beach, warmed by our hibachi coals and oblivious to the social climate around us. ◾

GRILLED BANANA MUFFINS

The natural sugar of the bananas caramelizes on the grill and makes the muffins praline-sweet. A perfect complement to too many mimosas.

1¹/₃ cups unsifted all-purpose flour
2¹/₂ teaspoons baking powder
¹/₄ teaspoon salt
2 very ripe bananas, mashed
²/₃ cup lightly packed dark brown sugar
¹/₃ cup orange or apple juice
1 cup vanilla yogurt
2 cups bran flakes
¹/₂ teaspoon nutmeg
¹/₄ cup slivered almonds

Recycling at its very best—butter transported, served, and stored in an old baby food jar.

Butter and flour 8 or 10 cups of a muffin pan. (These muffins are too sticky for paper or foil muffin cups.) Preheat the oven to 350° F.

In a large bowl mix together all the ingredients and stir with a wooden spoon until well blended but still slightly lumpy. Evenly divide the batter between all of the muffin cups (an ice cream scoop is incredibly useful for tasks like this).

Place the muffin pan on the middle rack of the oven and bake for 12 to 15 minutes, or until tops are golden. If you don't have a glass oven door, limit the times you open your oven door, and do so only in the last few minutes of baking and only if you have to. Let the muffins cool in the pan for about 5 to 10 minutes, then remove to a rack to finish cooling.

To grill, cut the muffins in half horizontally and spread the halves with a little (or a lot of) butter. Place them directly on the grill for about 3 to 4 minutes until they are toasted.

Makes 8 to 10 muffins

GRILLED ORANGE MUFFINS

Like Grilled Banana Muffins, these are prepared in just one bowl and the muffin pan, baked ahead of time, and grilled at the beach. I usually blend all of the wet ingredients in the food processor, then fold in the dry ingredients and the currants by hand.

1¹/₂ cups all-purpose flour
1 teaspoon baking soda
1 teaspoon baking powder
¹/₂ teaspoon salt
1 orange, grated, peeled, quartered, and seeds removed
6 tablespoons unsalted butter, room temperature
¹/₃ cup orange juice
³/₄ cup sugar
1 egg
¹/₂ cup currants or raisins

Butter and flour a 10- or 12-cup muffin pan. Preheat the oven to 400° F.

Sift together the flour, baking soda, baking powder, and salt. In a separate bowl, mash the orange quarters, and cream together with the butter. Fold in the grated orange peel, orange juice, sugar, and egg. Fold together with the dry ingredients and mix well. Fold in the currants or raisins and divide the batter evenly into the prepared muffin cups.

Bake on the middle rack of the oven for 12 to 15 minutes or until the tops are golden. To grill, see Grilled Banana Muffins, page 58.

Makes 10 to 12 muffins

GRILLED SAUSAGES

This is optional, for meat lovers only.

1 pound sweet Italian sausage

To grill, pierce with a fork so sausages do not burst. Grill over hot coals for 15 to 30 minutes, or until juices run clear.

MINTED MELON SALAD

If served at home instead of the beach, this colorful fruit salad may be chilled in the freezer for about 20 to 30 minutes before serving. The alcohol in the Triple Sec prevents it from freezing, but don't leave it there overnight.

5 cups of cut up or balled assorted seasonal melon (such as crenshaw, casaba, watermelon, cantaloupe, honeydew)
3 tablespoons chopped fresh mint leaves
2 (or more) ounces Cointreau or Triple Sec

In a large bowl, combine the melon and the mint leaves. Liberally pour on the liqueur and toss.

Makes 5 cups

WHAT GOES AROUND COMES AROUND

About once a year I begin to think that it's time I got around to repaying all those hospitable friends who have invited me to their homes so many times. At first the thought excites me and I start drawing up long lists of friends, mixing and matching according to who will eat meat and who will eat fish. Then I rearrange each list to accommodate who happens to be getting along with whom at the time, trying to separate the exes from the currents. Very quickly the idea of entertaining becomes more of an ordeal than an event as I mentally organize six or eight intimate dinners, all with different menus. I come to my senses and ultimately decide on just one or two larger gatherings with friends of diverse preferences and histories. If sparks fly...I just hope I get a ringside seat!

MENU

Seafood Paella

Herbed French Bread

Dark Green Salad with Lemon-Chive Vinaigrette

Rum Cake

The urge to entertain eight or ten people in a small apartment has never loomed large on my horizon of hospitality, especially since I own only six actual dining chairs, and one step-stool. I usually just serve buffet-style right from the stove and let everyone take a place on

the couch, the floor, or somewhere in between. Somehow this takes the nasty edge of formality right off the entire evening.

In most cases, the deepest wound of entertaining is the one inflicted on your wallet (and it's also the one that leaves the worst scars), so it's sometimes best to serve something that will affordably satiate more people than you're used to and still leave your Christmas Club intact.

Paella bridges the gap. Served in one big bowl or even the stockpot in which it's made, it is cost-efficient and delicious. I like to accompany paella with a large salad that has a heavy vegetable-to-lettuce ratio. This way vegetarians can make a meal out of the salad and not have to spend the entire meal sorting the fish from the grains of rice on their plates.

And remember, wine comes in gallon jugs in a variety of colors. ■

A meal for the masses can still have panache.

SEAFOOD PAELLA

Like a giant pot of spaghetti, paella can affordably feed many friends, and the shrimps, lobster, and clams that you have so judiciously placed on top won't make it look like you've pinched pennies till they've screamed. Should there be any left over, it can be refrigerated and reheated slowly over a low heat and splashed with some white wine.

$1/4$ cup good olive oil
2 medium yellow onions, chopped
3 leeks, white and some green part, coarsely chopped
4 large tomatoes, peeled, seeded, and chopped
1 14-ounce can artichoke hearts, drained, then halved
3 medium bell peppers, seeded and cut into $1/2$-inch strips
$5^1/2$ cups chicken or vegetable stock

Add 1 cup of the stock and bring to a simmer. Add the rice, simmer for 5 minutes, and then add the garlic and parsley.

Add the remaining stock, clams, and shrimp and continue cooking, covered, for 15 or 20 minutes or until all the stock is absorbed, the clams have opened, and the shrimp is pink.

Add the lobster parts, peas, and saffron. Season with salt and pepper to taste, stir, and let stand for 5 minutes. Discard any clams that have not opened and serve from the paella pan.

Serves 8

HERBED FRENCH BREAD

Simply by adding some melted butter and some fresh, or even dried, herbs this plain loaf becomes something that looks like you've made a profound effort...but, of course, you haven't.

2 tablespoons unsalted butter
2 garlic cloves, minced
2 tablespoons chopped fresh rosemary, or any combination of your favorite fresh or dried herbs
3 tablespoons good olive oil
1 loaf French bread

Melt the butter in a small saucepan over medium heat. Add the garlic and cook until lightly golden and fragrant. Stir in the rosemary or other herbs and the olive oil, and remove the saucepan from the heat.

Slice the French bread vertically, but not all the way through, leaving the loaf intact. Brush the butter mixture into the slices and place the loaf on a cookie sheet.

Preheat the broiler.

Toast the bread under the broiler just long enough to heat the bread and crisp the edges. Serve immediately.

Serves 8

1 pound (3 cups) raw long grain rice
4 garlic cloves, minced
2 tablespoons chopped fresh parsley
12 cherrystone clams, scrubbed in cold water
1 pound medium shrimp, peeled and deveined
1 1½-pound lobster cooked and cut into parts (claws and tails split, body discarded)
½ cup frozen peas
½ teaspoon saffron threads
Salt and pepper

In a large stockpot, heat the oil over medium heat. Add the onions and leeks and continue cooking until onions are translucent. Lower the heat and stir in the tomatoes. Fold in the artichoke hearts and the peppers, stirring constantly.

Here the paella saga begins, above. *Empty the vegetable drawer for the salad,* left.

DARK GREEN SALAD WITH LEMON-CHIVE VINAIGRETTE

This salad has broken a lot of friends of their iceberg lettuce habit. I save the (aptly named) pallid iceberg for exclusive use in the hamster's cage.

5 cups assorted dark greens (spinach, romaine, arugula, red leaf lettuce)
8 tablespoons extra virgin olive oil
4 tablespoons red wine vinegar, or to taste
Juice of 1 lemon
$1/4$ teaspoon Tabasco sauce
Grated peel of 1 lemon
3 tablespoons chopped fresh chives
Salt and pepper

Wash and dry the greens thoroughly and tear the leaves into smaller pieces.

In a small bowl, whisk together the oil, vinegar, lemon juice, and Tabasco until emulsified. Stir in the lemon peel and chives. Season with salt and pepper to taste. Pour over the greens and toss to coat.

Serve immediately.

Serves 8

RUM CAKE

This is a great recipe for the make-ahead file. Tightly covered, the cake will last a few days in the refrigerator. If it gets dry, refresh individual slices with a teaspoon of rum.

$1^1/2$ cups butter (3 sticks), at room temperature
$1^1/2$ cups sugar
1 teaspoon vanilla extract
2 eggs, plus 2 egg yolks
3 cups all-purpose flour
2 teaspoons baking powder
$1/2$ teaspoon salt
1 cup heavy cream or milk
$3/4$ cup dark rum
Grated peel of 1 lemon
Juice of 1 lemon
$1/4$ cup confectioner's sugar, measured without sifting
2 cups seasonal berries
Fresh mint leaves

Preheat the oven to 350° F.

Butter and flour a 10-inch Bundt or tube cake pan.

In a large mixing bowl, whip the butter with an electric beater or wooden spoon until it is creamy, then blend in the sugar, vanilla, eggs, and yolks. Beat until well blended.

In a separate bowl, sift together the flour, baking powder, and salt. Gradually add the dry ingredients to the butter mixture alternately with the heavy cream until smooth. Stir in the rum, then add both the grated lemon peel and the lemon juice.

Pour the mixture into the prepared cake pan and bake for 40 to 45 minutes or until the cake tests done. (The top should crack.)

Allow the cake to cool in the pan for 10 minutes, then turn onto a rack and remove the pan. Once the cake has cooled completely, dust with the confectioner's sugar and garnish with the berries and mint leaves.

Serves 10 to 12

With just a few shakes of confectioner's sugar, a few loose berries, and some mint leaves, the average cake looks like an event.

CHINESE TAKE-IN

My love of ethnic foods comes not from traveling the world over, or from eating in the most renowned restaurants. Rather it springs from an appreciation of take-out, an appreciation refined by years of skillful dialing. Indeed the telephone is as mighty a kitchen tool as any

food processor or automatic dishwasher. The beauty of take-out foods is self-evident. All you have to do is call, open the door, empty the box on your plate, chew, swallow, throw out the box, and good night. Needless to say there will be

occasions when you empty the box and wonder, Where did this come from? Or, Did I order *this*? Or, after the meal, Why am I experiencing a thirst known only to wanderers of the desert? Rather than combat the effects of MSG and too much sodium, try re-creating one of these meals at home. Most of the ingredients are available in their purest form at local grocers. The meal here is certainly worth the extra effort, and most of it can be prepared beforehand, like maybe in the

MENU
....
*Hot and Spicy
Flank Steak*

*Carrots in Black Bean
and Honey Sauce*

Cold Sesame Noodles

Fried Bananas

morning before fatigue fells your ambition. It is good to start a collection of Oriental spices.

Initially, they might seem unfamiliar, but after a few memorable meals they will seem as

user friendly as peanut butter and jelly. ■

HOT AND SPICY FLANK STEAK

All of the foreign-sounding spices listed below should be available in the dried herb and spice aisle of the supermarket. If not, try a gourmet store or Asian market.

    1-pound flank steak
    3 tablespoons sesame oil
    3 tablespoons rice wine vinegar
    3 tablespoons soy sauce
    4–5 coriander seeds, crushed (optional)
    1 teaspoon Five Spice powder
    1 garlic clove, minced
    1 teaspoon sugar
    1 teaspoon hot and spicy oil
    Juice of 1 orange, or $1/4$ cup orange juice
    1 pod star anise

Pierce the steak all over on both sides with a sharp fork and place in an ovenproof glass dish or baking pan.

In a large bowl, combine the remaining ingredients and blend well. Pour the marinade over the steak. Cover and chill for at least 2 hours, turning the steak several times.

Preheat the broiler. Remove the steak from the marinade and discard the marinade. Grill the steak at least 3 inches from the heat until the outside is crispy and the inside is medium rare and tender, about 7 to 10 minutes on each side. Slice very thin and serve immediately.

Serves 4

CARROTS IN BLACK BEAN AND HONEY SAUCE

Carrots need not be bland. Contrary to most people's basic culinary training, carrots are tastier sautéed than boiled or steamed.

    2 tablespoons vegetable oil
    3 cups julienned carrots (see Note)
    4 tablespoons black bean sauce (see Note)
    3 tablespoons honey
    Dash of hot pepper oil or soy sauce

In a large skillet over medium heat, heat the vegetable oil. Add the carrots and sauté until they are tender but still crunchy, about 5 minutes.

Stir in the black bean sauce, honey, and hot pepper oil or soy until well blended.

Serve immediately.

Serves 4

Note: Julienned carrots are cut into matchstick-sized pieces. Use the julienne blade of your food processor or a very sharp knife. Jars of black bean sauce can be found in the Asian foods section of the supermarket.

COLD SESAME NOODLES

You might be tempted to eat these as soon as they're cooked, but they are really best when chilled.

3/4 pound thin spaghetti
1 teaspoon vegetable oil
3 tablespoons sesame paste
2 tablespoons sesame oil
3 tablespoons light soy sauce or tamari
2 teaspoons rice wine vinegar
1-inch piece fresh ginger, peeled and finely
   minced
1 teaspoon red pepper flakes, or to taste
3–4 scallions, green part only, finely chopped

Cook the spaghetti according to the directions on the box. Drain and shake in the colander to get rid of most of the water. In a large bowl, toss the spaghetti with the vegetable oil to prevent the noodles from sticking together.

In a separate bowl, stir the sesame paste to smooth any lumps, then add the sesame oil and soy sauce and stir until well blended. Then add all the remaining ingredients except the scallions. Add the sauce to the cooked pasta and toss well to coat. Garnish with the scallions and chill until ready to serve.

Serves 3 to 4

FRIED BANANAS

Fried bananas also make a wonderful late-night snack.

1/4 cup all-purpose flour
3 tablespoons sugar
1 teaspoon cinnamon
1/8 teaspoon ground allspice
4 bananas, peeled and split lengthwise
3 tablespoons unsalted butter
Confectioner's sugar

In a bowl, mix together the flour, sugar, cinnamon, and allspice. Carefully dip the bananas into the flour mixture, making sure they are well coated.

In a large skillet over medium heat, melt half of the butter. Carefully place four of the banana halves in the butter and brown on both sides. Remove them to a plate and keep warm in the oven at its lowest setting. Repeat these steps with the remaining butter and bananas.

When ready to serve, dust with confectioner's sugar.

Serves 4

Barring any problems, you can usually have this entire dinner ready before even the fastest of delivery boys arrives, from the main course, opposite, to the Fried Bananas, above.

AN APARTMENT-DWELLER'S BARBECUE

If you live in an apartment with no outdoor space, the prospect of one day owning a grill may be right up there with digging a pool, building a garage, or dragging out the garbage. But just because you don't own a yard or all the responsibilities that go with it doesn't mean you have to sacrifice the pleasures of good grilled food.

MENU

*Grilled Jumbo Shrimp
with Yellow Tomatoes
and Peppers*

Simple Brown Rice

Black Beans

I once lived in an apartment that was so small it made Barbie's Camper look like the Palais Versailles. Nonetheless, like most apartments, it came equipped with a broiler. The broiler is not only an excellent surrogate for the outdoor grill, it is a cleaner, more efficient cooking environment. With a rack to allow most of the fat to drip away during cooking, the broiler produces results that, if not fat-free, are a lot healthier than fried or sautéed meals, where there is no choice but to serve the fat right along with food. Unlike backyard grilling, indoor broiling does not cause nimbocumulus clouds of semitoxic smoke to billow over the neighborhood. The percentage of error is smaller, as is the mess and the general aftermath. No petrified memories remain welded to your barbecue grill: just remove the pan, shut the door, and the horror is out of sight and out of mind until the next time.

I use the broiler a lot on weeknights, when I'm too lame after the workday to drag out the coals, flammables, and bug spray. I usually prepare something fairly simple like fish steaks spread with a little Dijon mustard and pepper or kabobs, which require some construction but little cooking. Then I always leave dessert up to whoever I've invited for dinner and was naive enough to ask if I needed anything. ■

With kabobs, most if not all of the work is in the construction.

GRILLED JUMBO SHRIMP WITH YELLOW TOMATOES AND PEPPERS

....

Soaking the wooden skewers in water for about 15 minutes makes serving a lot easier: the shrimp and vegetables will slide right off. If you can't find yellow peppers and tomatoes, change the color scheme to red.

4 teaspoons soy sauce
3 teaspoons honey
1 teaspoon minced garlic
1 teaspoon minced fresh ginger
2 large yellow bell peppers, cored, seeded, and cut into 1-inch pieces
2 pounds (about 16) jumbo shrimp (also called Australian prawns), peeled, deveined, and rinsed well
8 yellow cherry tomatoes or two large yellow tomatoes, cored and cut up
$1/4$ teaspoon red pepper flakes

In a small bowl, combine the soy sauce, honey, garlic, and ginger.

Using eight 12-inch skewers, arrange on each a slice of yellow pepper, a shrimp, then a tomato. Repeat this process until you have used up all of your vegetables and shrimp. Place the prepared skewers in a glass baking dish and pour the marinade over them. Sprinkle red pepper evenly over the skewers and chill, covered, for an hour, turning the skewers over two or three times.

Preheat the broiler. Liberally brush any excess marinade over the fish. Grill for 5 to 7 minutes on each side, or until the shrimp are pink and the vegetables are crispy. Serve immediately.

Serves 4

SIMPLE BROWN RICE

Brown rice is just as easy to make as the plain white rice we are all so familiar with. It now even comes in cooking bags that can be dropped right into a pot of boiling water and require absolutely no intelligence or skill, but then you can't use this delicious recipe.

2 tablespoons unsalted butter
$1/2$ cup chopped celery
$1/2$ cup chopped carrots
2 cups water
2 cups dry white wine
1 teaspoon vegetable oil
Salt and pepper
2 cups raw brown rice

Melt the butter in a large saucepan over medium heat. Add the celery and carrots and cook the vegetables for about 5 minutes or until they become tender. Stir in the water and the wine. Raise the heat and bring to a rolling boil. Add the oil and salt and pepper, to taste.

Pour in the rice and return to a boil, then lower the heat and simmer, covered, for 45 minutes, or until all the water has been absorbed. Serve immediately.

Serves 4

BLACK BEANS

Never mind their silly reputation, beans are a great source of protein, especially when served with fish and generous amounts of brown rice.

1 garlic clove, minced
1 teaspoon vegetable oil
1 medium red onion, sliced into rings
2 16-ounce cans black beans, drained and rinsed well
$1/4$ teaspoon cayenne pepper
Salt and pepper

In a large skillet over medium heat, sauté the garlic in the oil until golden. Add the onion rings and sauté until they have wilted. Stir in the beans and mix well. Stir in the cayenne pepper and salt and pepper to taste and remove the pan from the heat. Serve immediately.

Serves 4

LUNCH GUESTS: INVITED OR OTHERWISE

There was a knock at the door, followed by the chilling announcement, "Hi, we were just in the neighborhood." The cupboards were bare, and I had little more to serve for lunch than the milk of human kindness, which always left sort of a funny taste in my mouth any-

way. After closer inspection of refrigerator and pantry, I approached this challenge with the same hesitant determination as I do bathing the dog. But forty-five minutes later, this lunch (sans dessert, which you can whip up in advance if your guests are courteous enough to give warning) was on the table.

MENU

Pasta Aglio e Olio

Bruschetta

Bibb Lettuce and
Blue Cheese Salad

Lemon Ice

It's not that I'm better prepared than a Boy Scout. It's simply that the ingredients here are not at all exotic and should be kept on hand for just such "drop-in" occasions. Don't ask me to pronounce it—every time I've asked, the waiter has corrected me and pronounced it his own way—but Pasta Aglio e Olio is simply cooked spaghetti or linguini with sautéed garlic and olive oil. The variations start from there. Sun-dried

LUNCH GUESTS: INVITED OR OTHERWISE   **77**

tomatoes, sliced mushrooms, black olives, and so on can embellish your signature meal. Pasta Aglio e Olio is served in most Italian restaurants as a side dish to nonpasta main courses. Most people don't know to ask and end up with spaghetti topped with the house marinara, which has often been delivered to the restaurant kitchen in a very large industrial-looking can. ■

As easy to prepare as opening a jar of sauce, Pasta Aglio e Olio is what Italians really eat.

PASTA AGLIO E OLIO

Some folks like to slap their pasta against the wall to see if it sticks. Actually, stickiness means that only the outside of the noodle is cooked and the starch is gluing it to the wall. Spare your kitchen's paint job: fish a few noodles out of the boiling water and chew.

1½ pounds linguini or spaghetti
½ cup extra virgin olive oil
1 dried chili pepper
4–5 garlic cloves, coarsely chopped
Salt and pepper
6 tablespoons chopped fresh parsley
Grated Parmesan, Romano, or Asiago cheese

Cook the spaghetti according to the package directions, drain well, transfer to a large bowl, and toss with 2 tablespoons of the oil.

In a large skillet, heat the remaining oil with the chili pepper over medium heat until the pepper begins to brown. Add the chopped garlic to the heated oil and sauté just until it is lightly browned. (This shouldn't take a minute.)

Remove the skillet from the heat and discard the pepper. Toss half of the oil and garlic with the cooked pasta. Divide the pasta evenly in bowls and top each serving with the rest of the oil and garlic. Add salt and pepper to taste. Garnish with spoonfuls of the chopped parsley. Serve immediately with lots of freshly grated cheese.

Serves 4

BRUSCHETTA

Having a good bottle of olive oil around the house really pays off in this simple recipe. I almost always chop garlic by hand for the best texture.

2¹/₂ cups chopped and seeded fresh Italian
    plum tomatoes
1 small yellow onion, chopped
¹/₄ cup chopped fresh basil
¹/₄ cup sliced or chopped pitted black olives
2 garlic cloves, finely minced
¹/₂ teaspoon salt
¹/₄ cup extra virgin olive oil
8–10 slices toasted semolina bread (see Note)
Cracked or coarsely ground black pepper

In a large bowl, toss together the tomatoes, onion, basil, olives, garlic, and salt. Pour in the oil and let stand for an hour. Spoon over the toasted bread and sprinkle with black pepper. Serve immediately.

Serves 4 to 6

Note: Semolina bread is a long yellowish loaf of Italian bread sometimes coated with sesame seeds; it's most associated with Italian take-out.

Bruschetta is one of those dishes you can serve as an hors d'oeuvre, a side dish, or a salad— whenever you get it to the table.

BIBB LETTUCE AND BLUE CHEESE SALAD

This salad has only a few simple ingredients and an even simpler dressing. If you resent having to measure, memorize this formula: 3, 2, 1 (3 parts olive oil, 2 parts vinegar, and 1 part soy sauce).

4 cups Bibb, Boston, or baby lettuce, rinsed
    and dried
¹/₂ cup crumbled blue cheese
¹/₈ cup coarsely chopped walnuts
1 tablespoon (3 teaspoons) extra virgin
    olive oil
2 teaspoons red wine vinegar
1 teaspoon soy sauce

Tear the lettuce leaves into a salad bowl and add the crumbled cheese and walnuts. Pour the olive oil evenly over the salad, then pour in the vinegar and the soy sauce. Toss to coat. (This salad should not be drenched in dressing, so hold back if it looks too wet.) Serve the salad immediately.

Serves 4

LEMON ICE

Lemon Ice can be made fairly quickly and can be stored in the freezer for up to two weeks, as long as it is in an air-tight container.

2 cups fresh lemon juice
1¹/₂ cups sugar
1¹/₂ cups heavy cream
Grated peel of 2 lemons
¹/₂ cup water
Lemon slices or fresh mint leaves to garnish

Puree all of the ingredients in a food processor and freeze in the food processor bowl for at least 2 hours, or until solid. Scoop out with an ice cream scoop or spoon that has been dipped in warm water. Before serving, garnish with lemon slices or fresh mint leaves.

T, MY NAME IS TURKEY (THANKSGIVING)

Thanksgiving is my favorite holiday of the entire year. It is based completely on overindul-gence—perhaps the only occasion when the most you are required to do is eat too much, watch too much TV, then nap like a narcoleptic.

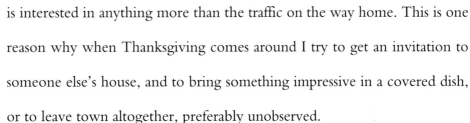

This is, of course, unless this occasion happens to take place in your house and you have to do all the cooking and cleaning up. Sure, everyone says they will help, but my experience has been that once the fork hits the plate for the last time no one is interested in anything more than the traffic on the way home. This is one reason why when Thanksgiving comes around I try to get an invitation to someone else's house, and to bring something impressive in a covered dish, or to leave town altogether, preferably unobserved.

Over the past several years I must admit I have not had much luck in this regard. The night before Thanksgiving my family and friends have been

MENU

*Roast Turkey
and Gravy*

*Corn Bread
and Sausage Stuffing*

*Onions in
Champagne Sauce*

Creamed Spinach

Cranberry Sorbet

Pecan Pie

*Oatmeal-Prune
Cookies*

known to surround my house, like Comanches circling the wagon train, in hopes of getting invited in for all of those great Thanksgiving victuals. Halfway between the house and the garage I'm weakened by their hungered expressions, drop my overnight bag, and hesitantly invite them all in.

My second mistake has been to use Thanksgiving as a vehicle to expand my family's ever-narrowing palate by trying to come up with something new each year to replace something old—preferably something old that I was never really fond of myself. This year, I've decided to abandon canned cranberry jelly, which just wriggles out of the can and onto the plate all by itself, in favor of an easy-to-make cranberry sorbet, served just after the turkey but before dessert. Making it a separate course is sophisticated and should make everyone sit up, finally put their napkins in their respective laps, and pretend to know what fork does what. ◼

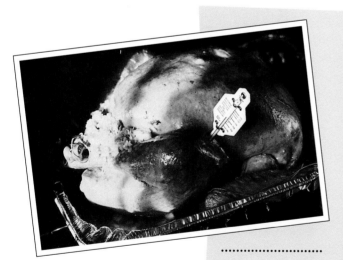

Rather than waiting around for a pop-up timer, try a meat thermometer. It relieves a lot of the stress and limits the times you open the oven.

ROAST TURKEY AND GRAVY

Like remedies for the common cold, methods of roasting the perfect Thanksgiving turkey are numerous. Sadly, this is not an exact science, and the results are governed by factors like oven size, temperature accuracy, and by frozen, thawed, or fresh. I find I have the most success if I remember to limit the number of times I open the oven door. The turkey should be loosely stuffed and centered in the oven. A correctly defrosted plump turkey of 12 to 15 pounds should only take about 4 hours to roast. The best way to test for doneness is with an accurate meat thermometer. Unlike wiggling legs, thermometers don't lie. Baste once an hour at the most. Any more than this and you have bent the door-opening rule. Frozen turkeys should begin defrosting in their wrappings in the refrigerator two days before Thanksgiving.

1 12–15 pound turkey, giblets, neck, and livers removed (and possibly discarded)
1/4 pound (1 stick) unsalted butter
1 cup dry white wine
Salt and pepper

Preheat the oven to 425° F.

Thoroughly rinse the turkey both inside and out. Rub the skin with the butter. Season with salt and pepper. Make a loop out of 3 feet of kitchen string by tying both ends together. Lay this across the roasting pan rack. Loosely stuff, then truss (tie up any loose legs or skin) the turkey and carefully place it in the center of the pan. (Clean the work surface and hands with warm sudsy water or lemon juice.)

Reduce the oven heat to 350° F. Add 1/2 inch of water to the bottom of the roasting pan. Roast the turkey uncovered, basting only once an hour with the white wine, turning the roasting pan 180 degrees each time. After 2 1/2 to 3 hours, tent the bird with aluminum foil to prevent the skin from burning and baste with the pan drippings. Test for doneness with a meat thermometer; it should read 185° to 190° F.

When roasting is complete, remove the turkey from the oven. Lift the turkey out of the roasting pan and onto the serving dish, using the string as handles. Before carving, let the turkey stand 20 minutes to settle the juices. It will still be hot enough to serve.

Serves 12 to 15

GRAVY

Gravy is easily ruined, and making gravy can be quite character building for the novice. Look failure right in the face and make it over again, rather than rely on the blatantly gelatinous store-bought kind.

Pan drippings from the turkey pan
Flour (no more than 3 tablespoons)
1–1 1/2 cups milk, light cream, or white wine
Salt and pepper

Once the turkey and rack have been removed from the pan, pour off the fat from the drippings. Pour the drippings into a medium saucepan, scraping the bottom of the pan to loosen, and heat over low or medium heat.

Measuring teaspoon by teaspoon, sprinkle in the flour, stirring constantly with a wooden spoon to prevent lumps until the gravy has thickened and the flour has lost its starchy taste. Still stirring, start adding small amounts of milk, cream, or white wine, until thickened and well blended. Do not flatten the taste of the gravy by adding too much liquid. You will know when you have gone too far, because you will be constantly tasting and correcting the seasonings. If you have it, a teaspoon of Dijon mustard might help revive the taste.

Makes 1 1/2 to 2 cups gravy

*A very still life
of Cranberry
Sorbet,* **above.**
*On Thanksgiving,
you'll use every dish
in the house,* **right.**
*Get the guests to
wash them.*

CORN BREAD AND SAUSAGE STUFFING

The best stuffings are made by editorializing on a basic recipe and by using up any appropriate ingredients found in the spice cabinet or vegetable drawer of the refrigerator.

1/2 (1 stick) cup unsalted butter
2 stalks celery, chopped
1 medium onion, chopped
2 Granny Smith apples, peeled, cored, and diced
1 pound Italian sweet sausage, cooked, drained, and crumbled
1 cup chopped pecans
1 10-ounce package frozen whole kernel corn
1 cup dry white wine or dry sherry
1/2 teaspoon each dried thyme, sage, and parsley
6 cups crumbled corn bread (recipe follows)

....
A signature bird dressing, above, will be remembered long after the mess on the stove top is forgotten. Virgin Thanksgiving plates, opposite, await their burden.

In a large stockpot, melt the butter over medium heat. Stir in the celery and onion and sauté until they are translucent. Add the apples, sausage, and pecans, and stir to mix well. Break up and add the frozen corn and stir again. Then add the wine or sherry and seasonings. Turn off the heat and fold in the corn bread. See turkey recipe (page 82) for stuffing and roasting instructions.

Makes about 8 cups

CORN BREAD

1 1/4 cups yellow cornmeal
3/4 cup unsifted flour
4 teaspoons baking powder
1/2 teaspoon salt
1 teaspoon sugar
1 cup milk or heavy cream
1 egg, lightly beaten
1 tablespoon unsalted butter

Preheat the oven to 400° F. Place a 9-inch ovenproof skillet or pie plate in the oven while it preheats.

In a large bowl, mix together the cornmeal, flour, baking powder, salt, and sugar. Add the milk and egg and mix well to make a slightly lumpy batter.

When the oven is preheated, remove the skillet and add the butter. Brush the butter around the skillet to coat the entire surface. Pour the batter in the skillet. Bake for 20 to 25 minutes. Let the corn bread cool in the skillet for 10 minutes, then remove to a rack to finish cooling.

Makes about 6 cups, crumbled

In a colander drain the liquid from the onions and discard. Stir the onions into the champagne sauce until well blended. Serve immediately.

Makes about 6 cups

CREAMED SPINACH

This is as green as it gets on Thanksgiving. Creamed Spinach is best when made ahead and reheated just before serving.

2 tablespoons unsalted butter
1 garlic clove, minced
2 leeks, green part only, chopped
2 10-ounce packages frozen leaf spinach,
  thawed and chopped
1/4 cup heavy cream
2 cups sour cream
1/4 teaspoon nutmeg
Salt and pepper

Preheat the oven to 400° F.

Melt the butter in a large saucepan over medium heat. Add the garlic and sauté until golden. Add the leeks and cook until wilted.

Drain the spinach of any excess moisture by pressing it into a colander. Don't go overboard; it needs some moisture to cook. Add the spinach to the garlic and leeks, then blend in the heavy cream. Fold in the sour cream. Season with nutmeg and salt and pepper to taste. Remove the pan from the heat.

Butter and flour an ovenproof dish. Pour the mixture into the prepared dish and smooth the top with the back of a wooden spoon. Bake for 20 to 25 minutes, or until the top is golden. Set the dish aside and reheat in a warm (200° to 250° F.) oven before serving.

Serves 6 to 8

ONIONS IN CHAMPAGNE SAUCE

This started out as regular old Creamed Onions, but one Thanksgiving morning, all alone with a leftover half bottle of champagne, some jarred onions, and my own elemental cooking skills, I invented this hybrid.

3 tablespoons unsalted butter
2 tablespoons unsifted flour
3/4 cup heavy cream
1 cup champagne (flat is fine, but not sour)
1 teaspoon dried tarragon
4 12 1/4-ounce jars boiled onions
Salt and pepper

Melt the butter in a large saucepan over medium heat. Gradually sift in the flour, stirring often to avoid lumps, until the mixture is thick and bubbling. Gradually pour in the heavy cream and champagne. Simmer for a few minutes until the mixture thickens. Stir in the tarragon.

Save yourself the trouble and expense of flower arrangements by using the raw materials left over from the meal, left. All good Thanksgivings must come to an end—with pie, above.

CRANBERRY SORBET

Not only does Cranberry Sorbet clear the palate, but it makes the sometimes awkward transition from dinner to dessert rather graceful.

1^1/$_2$ cups (12 ounces) cranberries
1^1/$_2$ cups water
^{3}/$_4$ cup sugar
1^1/$_2$ teaspoons minced fresh ginger
^{3}/$_4$ cup orange juice
2 tablespoons Triple Sec or Cointreau

Rinse the cranberries and remove any stems.

Bring the water and sugar to a boil in a medium saucepan, then add the cranberries and the ginger to the syrup. Reduce the heat and simmer about 15 minutes, or until the berries have popped their skins. Remove from the heat and let stand to cool about 15 minutes.

Puree the mixture in a food processor or blender, then strain it through a strainer or colander into a bowl. Discard the pulp. Stir the orange juice and liqueur into the cranberry puree. Pour 3/4 of the mixture into ice trays and freeze for several hours or overnight. Chill the remainder in the refrigerator. When the puree has frozen, combine the frozen and refrigerated mixtures in the food processor or blender, then freeze for at least an hour.

Serves 6

With no help from Mrs. Smith, the Crafts family pie-making tradition lives on, above and opposite.

PECAN PIE

I usually make this in a very shallow tin or aluminum pie plate that has lots of holes in the bottom. These perforated pans, exclusively available in great number at tag sales or thrift stores, ensure a nonsoggy bottom.

^{1}/$_2$ recipe A Very Basic Pie Crust (see page 25)
^{1}/$_3$ cup dark corn syrup
2 eggs
^{1}/$_2$ cup (1 stick) unsalted butter, melted
^{1}/$_2$ cup sugar
1 teaspoon vanilla extract
1 cup pecan halves

Preheat the oven to 375° F. Butter and flour a 9-inch pie plate. Roll out the pastry and line the prepared pie plate, finish the edges, and pierce the bottom of the crust all over with a fork.

In a large bowl, blend well the corn syrup, eggs, butter, sugar, and vanilla. Pour the mixture into the prepared pie crust and carefully arrange the pecan halves on top, starting from the outside and working in. Bake for 30 to 35 minutes or until the crust is golden and the pie has set. Let cool a bit and serve warm with vanilla ice cream.

Makes one 9-inch pie

OATMEAL-PRUNE COOKIES

These cookies are great to have around to serve with coffee. They cover every nutritional base, leave no stone unturned, and make it look like you've really tried.

1 cup pitted prunes
1½ cups unsifted flour, measured by dipping the cup into the flour and then leveling it off with a knife
1 teaspoon baking soda
½ teaspoon salt
½ teaspoon cinnamon
¼ teaspoon nutmeg
¾ cup (2½ sticks) unsalted butter, room temperature
8 ounces cream cheese, room temperature
1 teaspoon vanilla extract
1 egg
1 cup brown sugar, firmly packed
¼ cup granulated sugar
3 cups uncooked instant oatmeal
2 ounces slivered almonds

Place the prunes, flour, baking soda, salt, cinnamon, and nutmeg in the food processor. Pulse until the prunes are coarsely chopped and the other ingredients are well mixed. Empty this into a large bowl.

In the now-empty work bowl of the processor, combine the butter, cream cheese, vanilla, and egg and blend until smooth. Add both the sugars to the butter mixture and pulse again until well blended. Using a wooden spoon, add the butter mixture to the mixing bowl with the flour and fold together. Finally, add the oatmeal and almonds and mix well. Chill in a covered bowl for 1 hour.

Preheat the oven to 350° F. Drop the dough by the teaspoonful onto an ungreased cookie sheet and bake for 10 to 12 minutes. Allow the cookies to cool on the cookie sheet for 4 to 5 minutes, then remove to a rack to finish cooling.

Makes about 4 dozen cookies

CHRISTMAS: IT'S A SEMI-WONDERFUL LIFE

Once upon a time, on a December evening not so long ago, an old friend happened to call. After a few brief moments of holiday chatter she mentioned how nice it would be if her kids had a traditional gingerbread house for Christmas. I knew for a fact the only house her kids

wanted was one with cable, but I remembered when I was a kid, how every year my grandmother would send us a giant gingerbread house laminated with a generous array of gumdrops and candies and mortared with heaps of royal icing (nothing less than toxic by today's standards). Just before my friend hung up she very pointedly chided, "Nothing too much, just a Tudor or something." "No pool?" I quietly responded. Suddenly I was obliged and completely disinterested. But since I try never to fall back on a promise, least of all one made during the holidays, I bravely started in my valiant attempt to re-create Mar-a-Lago in gingerbread.

MENU

Roast Duck with Bourbon Sauce

La Mère's Baked Endive

Cabbage with Bacon and Almonds

Winter Vegetable Mash

Soffie's Scandinavian Pudding

After consulting a highly respected source, I mixed what I thought would be enough dough to construct a veritable Levittown of gingerbread tract homes. The small brown lump that appeared in the bottom of the mixing bowl sent me back to the recipe, and what to my wandering eye did appear, fine print that read "Merry Christmas to all, now make five times this amount!" After the first attempt I was able to piece together the roof and two side walls. With the help of some carpenter's wood glue and bent coat hangers, the house—dubbed the Gingerbread Garage by the few friends I allowed in the kitchen—now actually stood by itself, provided that no one came within ten or so feet of it.

Using candles is an easier and emotionally less expensive way to set the holiday table than with a gingerbread castle.

Weeks passed. My friend kept calling, excitedly checking on my progress, and each time I made up a more imaginative excuse. As Christmas drew closer I knew I would have to confront her with the ugly truth: there would be no gingerbread Tudor, never mind the gingerbread tennis court or gingerbread pool. On the few occasions that she has talked to me since then, she has never failed to mention the disappointment she and her children faced that Christmas morning. If it's true that we learn from our mistakes, I've realized the hard way that it is far easier to make plane reservations and leave town until after New Year's than it is to make a house of dough. Since that Christmas not so long ago, I have made my holiday plans as minimal as modern art, because less is even more at Christmastime. ∎

ROAST DUCK WITH BOURBON SAUCE

Whenever I make this, I'm usually pretty heavy-handed with the bourbon. No one has ever seemed to mind. If you do add too much and your sauce smells like it could easily catch fire, let it cook a little longer to evaporate the alcohol.

1 4–4$^{1}/_{2}$ pound duckling
Salt and pepper
1 cup honey
$^{3}/_{4}$ cup orange juice
$^{3}/_{4}$ cup bourbon, or to taste
1 teaspoon cornstarch

Preheat the oven to 425° F.

Remove the liver, neck, and gizzards from the cavity of the duck. Remove any excess visible fat from the duck and discard. Thoroughly rinse the duck with cold water, then rub inside and out with salt and pepper.

Place the duck on a rack in a roasting pan. Add $^{1}/_{2}$ inch of water to the base of the pan. Loosely tent the duck with aluminum foil and roast 45 minutes on the middle rack of the oven. Don't open the oven door.

Take the duck out of the oven and remove the foil. Brush the duck with about $^{1}/_{4}$ cup of the honey. Place the duck back in the oven, turn down the heat to 400° F., and roast uncovered for another 25 to 30 minutes, or until the juices run clear when the duck's thigh is pierced with a fork.

Meanwhile, back on the stove top…In a saucepan over medium heat bring the remaining honey, orange juice, and bourbon to a simmer. Gradually sprinkle in the cornstarch and let simmer for about 5 to 7 minutes, stirring often, until the sauce has thickened slightly. Remove the sauce from the heat and let stand a few minutes.

Remove the duck from the oven and brush liberally with some of the sauce. Reserve the rest of the sauce to be served on the side. Let the duck stand 10 minutes before serving.

Serves 3 to 4

*Christmas dinner is
served proudly
from the stove top,
above. Simple
cheese boards,
right, allow you
time for more press-
ing holiday matters,
like carousing with
your guests and
opening the gifts
they often bear.*

LA MÈRE'S BAKED ENDIVE

This recipe has been explained to me in three different languages, because it's a traditional family recipe from the Swiss side of my family, where languages abound, some understandable, some not. It is simple to make and has a high rate of success. Most important, it makes an impression and is a great confidence builder for inhibited cooks.

1 tablespoon extra virgin olive oil
Salt and white pepper
1 pound Belgian endive, trimmed and split in
    half lengthwise
1 cup heavy cream

Preheat the oven to 400° F.

Brush the inside of a 7$^{1}/_{2}$ x 11$^{3}/_{4}$-inch baking dish with the olive oil, then sprinkle with salt and white pepper. Place the endive halves in the baking dish. Pour the heavy cream over the endives and sprinkle with some more salt and pepper.

Bake for 20 to 25 minutes, turning the endives over once so that both sides are browned. Serve immediately.

Serves 4 to 6

*Like old Christmas
stockings and Bing
Crosby, candles
are a must.*

CABBAGE WITH BACON AND ALMONDS

I usually make two vegetable dishes at Christmas, preferably easy ones, and I serve them right from the stove, buffet-style.

1 small head cabbage, rinsed
5 strips lean slab bacon
1 garlic clove, coarsely chopped
2 ounces slivered almonds
1 cup dry white wine
Salt and pepper

Shred the cabbage as you would for slaw, using a food processor or a grater.

In a stockpot over medium heat cook the bacon until crispy. Remove to a paper towel to drain. Spoon off all but 2 tablespoons of the bacon fat from the stockpot. Add the garlic, and sauté until golden.

Reduce the heat, add the almonds, and cook until lightly browned. Then add the cabbage, the white wine, and salt and pepper to taste. Toss to coat and cook, covered, until the cabbage is wilted, about 8 to 10 minutes. Serve immediately.

Serves 6 to 8

WINTER VEGETABLE MASH

Any proportion of any or all of these winter vegetables can be used here. Finished, the mash should have the consistency of mashed potatoes. Lumps, of course, are optional.

6 cups water
1–1½ cups any combination of carrots, turnips, and rutabagas, peeled and cut into 1-inch pieces
2 Idaho or russet potatoes, peeled and cut into 1-inch pieces

1 large sweet potato, peeled and cut into 1-inch pieces
4 tablespoons (½ stick) unsalted butter, room temperature
4 ounces cream cheese, room temperature
½ teaspoon nutmeg
Salt and pepper

Bring the water to a rolling boil in a large stockpot over high heat. Add the cut-up carrots, turnips, rutabagas, and potatoes, and reduce heat. Cook gently until vegetables are tender when pierced with a fork, or about 20 minutes. Drain.

In a mixing bowl combine the butter, cream cheese, and nutmeg. Add the cooked vegetables and blend with a hand mixer to the desired consistency. Season with salt and pepper to taste. Serve immediately, or keep warm until ready to serve in a 200° to 250° F. oven.

Serves 6

Endive baked in a simple sauce lets the family know there will be no frozen vegetables this Christmas.

White Chocolate Stars,
left, *put a humble
pudding in a holiday
mood. Christmas nog,*
above, *is enhanced
with swirls of nutmeg,
cinnamon, and far
too much rum.*

SOFFIE'S SCANDINAVIAN PUDDING

My non-Scandinavian friend Soffie stuffed this recipe in my pocket one day. On a small scrap of paper she had scribbled "Scandinavian Pudding" and a list of ingredients, but had given no cooking instructions or amounts. After a few brave attempts, I was able to serve her this simple pudding, rich with sour cream. It can be garnished with White Chocolate Stars (recipe follows) or, if you feel less motivated, berries, mint leaves, or a shake of either cinnamon or nutmeg.

2 cups heavy cream
1 cup sugar
1 teaspoon vanilla
2 cups sour cream
1 package unflavored gelatin

In a medium saucepan over a low flame add the heavy cream and sugar. Simmer until all the sugar has melted. Do not boil. Remove the saucepan from the heat and let cool to room temperature.

In a bowl, blend the vanilla and sour cream. Beat into the cooled heavy cream mixture, then gradually sift in the gelatin, stirring often. Divide the mixture evenly among six glasses or dessert cups and chill for at least 1 hour.

Serves 6

Matching flatware, plates, and sometimes dining chairs is just another "work in progress."

WHITE CHOCOLATE STARS

4 ounces white chocolate

In a double boiler over low heat, slowly melt the chocolate, stirring constantly. When the chocolate is smooth, pour it into a pastry bag with a number 8 tip, or make a cone out of wax paper, tape it together, and snip off the end $1/8$-inch from the tip.

Place a sheet of wax paper on a cookie sheet, and draw stars onto it by squeezing the warm chocolate through the bag or paper cone. Chill the stars for at least 20 minutes. When ready to use, carefully peel the wax paper away from the stars—not the stars from the paper, or they will break. Place them on top of the pudding.

Makes 10 stars

CREATIVE LEFTOVERS

In my pantry on an average day the Slim-Fast sits proudly alongside the Pepperidge Farm cookies. The refrigerator houses an old doggie bag and the mandatory open box of baking soda. Like everyone else, I'm notoriously unprepared. When it comes time for late-night

snacking I may find only a jar of Dijon mustard and those little packages of soy sauce the Chinese restaurant has sent too many of. My grocery shopping is short-term and my consumption immediate. No great leftovers…this isn't Mom's.

Ironically, the key to creative leftovers is careful preparation. This is just another of the harsh realities of single living and recreational consumption. When it's 3 A.M. and the pain of late-night hunger has you banging down the refrigerator door, it's not the time to haul out the stockpot. However, if you plan ahead and make a large pot of soup, you will enjoy a few great lunches and dinners during the week and have enough surplus to satisfy any insomniac desires that overwhelm you during the night. It's a lot more fun dining solo by the light of the silvery refrigerator bulb than it is counting sheep anyway. ∎

MENU

Corn and Optional Lobster or Shrimp Soup

Gruyère Toasts with Puree of Sun-Dried Tomatoes

CORN AND OPTIONAL LOBSTER OR SHRIMP SOUP

There are foods said to be best the day after. Like stews, meatloaf, and most other soups, this is one of them. It is easily heated on the stove top over a medium flame. Don't use the microwave: This makes it far too hot to eat before the sun rises.

3 tablespoons vegetable oil
1 medium onion, chopped
1–2 jalapeño peppers, finely minced
3 cups chicken or vegetable stock (canned is okay)
1 16-ounce package (4 cups) frozen whole kernel corn, thawed
4 tablespoons unsifted all-purpose flour
1 medium red bell pepper, cored and diced
2–3 stalks celery, diced
3 cups milk or light cream

$1/2$ teaspoon cumin
$1/4$ teaspoon chili powder
Pinch of cayenne pepper
2 tablespoons chopped fresh cilantro
Salt and pepper to taste
8 ounces cooked lobster meat or shrimp (optional)

In a stockpot, heat the oil over medium heat, add the onion and the jalapeño and cook until onions are wilted.

Add the stock and 3 cups of the corn. Raise the heat and bring the mixture to a gentle boil, then remove the pot from the heat and allow the soup to cool for 15 minutes. In a food processor, puree $1/4$ of the soup at a time, adding a tablespoon of flour each time and pureeing until smooth.

Return the soup to the stockpot; add the bell pepper, celery, milk, cumin, chili powder, cayenne, and bring to a simmer over medium heat. Simmer until the celery has wilted and the pepper is soft, about five minutes. Add the cilantro, salt and pepper, and remove the pot from the heat.

Stir in the lobster, if using, and let stand for 5 to 10 minutes. Serve today or tomorrow, or freeze for up to two weeks and reheat.

Makes 8 cups

GRUYÈRE TOASTS WITH PUREE OF SUN-DRIED TOMATOES

This is just a fancy name for a grilled cheese sandwich.

4 ounces Gruyère cheese, cut into thin slices
2–3 slices Italian or any thickly sliced bread
2 teaspoons of Puree of Sun-Dried Tomatoes
 (recipe follows) or Dijon mustard

Preheat the broiler.
Place the cheese slices on top of the bread and toast under the broiler until the cheese has melted and the toast edges are crisp. Top with the Puree of Sun-Dried Tomatoes or Dijon mustard. Serve immediately.

Serves 2

PUREE OF SUN-DRIED TOMATOES

Purchase dried tomatoes rather than the pricey alternative, which are packed in oil.

1 cup dry sun-dried tomatoes
2–3 garlic cloves
1 teaspoon capers, drained, or 3 anchovy fillets
1/4 cup extra virgin olive oil

In a large saucepan, bring 4 cups of water to a rapid boil. Add the tomatoes to the boiling water and stir. Cook for a minute or two, just long enough to soften the tomatoes.

Drain the tomatoes. In a food processor puree the tomatoes, garlic, and capers, gradually adding the oil in three stages until the mixture is smooth.

Store tightly covered.

Makes about 1 1/2 cups

SHORT ON BRAINS BUT A TERRIFIC MAIN COURSE

The ability to cook just one great meal can be as erotically stimulating to a potential date, lover, or friend as any muscle car, trendy apartment, or da Vinci-esque etchings. You could be weighed down by imitation gold jewelry or marinated in cheap cologne—a gesture as

MENU

Glenn's Sautéed Scallops in Sweet Vermouth

Asparagus with Orange Hollandaise Sauce

Cous Cous

simple and unassuming as a good meal served in a relaxed and preferably candlelit setting obscures all other shortcomings, and it won't be due to the lack of light. The idea here is to impress that certain someone with a certain something that is a little out of the ordinary but very simple to prepare. The illusion is created by the kind of food and wine you serve, the music you select, and the pace at which you time the advances.

First, the food: Scallops, an uncommon selection but once you have mastered this simple technique, your dinner companion will wonder if you have ever studied abroad; Orange Hollandaise Sauce, carefully blended by hand and not squeezed from an envelope (you might want to mention that); and Cous Cous, not your average Macaroni Helper. It's romantic dishes like these that will make your guest look right past the salt and pepper and stare deeply into your eyes. Dessert…who knows? You might want to feed each other fresh grapes and champagne, go for a long walk hand in hand for an ice cream cone, call it a night, or retire together to a more secluded part of the house. ◼

....
"Was it in Tahiti? Were we on the Nile?"

GLENN'S SAUTÉED SCALLOPS IN SWEET VERMOUTH
....

In this case, serving the historically romantic oyster would be too obvious. Best to stick with the more subliminal scallop.

1 pound sea scallops
1 tablespoon olive oil
1 tablespoon unsalted butter
1–2 medium garlic cloves, minced
2–3 tablespoons sweet vermouth
1 teaspoon water

Gently rinse the scallops well under cold water and pat them dry between paper towels.

In a large skillet, heat the oil and melt the butter over medium heat. Add the garlic and cook until lightly golden. Add the scallops and cook until they are golden, but not cooked all the way through, about 4 minutes.

Add the vermouth and the water to the sauce. Lower the heat and finish cooking until the scallops are crisp on the outside and tender on the inside, about 2 or 3 minutes more. Serve immediately.

Serves 2

STEAMED ASPARAGUS WITH ORANGE HOLLANDAISE SAUCE

1 bunch thin asparagus (about 15 stalks)
Orange Hollandaise Sauce (recipe follows)

Trim away any tough ends and wash the asparagus thoroughly. Place into a steamer basket over boiling water and steam for about 5 minutes, or until the stalks are firm but can be pierced easily with a fork. Drain and serve with Orange Hollandaise Sauce.

Serves 2 to 4

ORANGE HOLLANDAISE SAUCE

The tricky part about hollandaise is that eggs will scramble if they get too hot too fast. As with seduction, proceed slowly and gently. If you fail, throw the mess out and start over immediately.

$1/2$ cup (1 stick) unsalted butter
Juice of 1 orange
3 egg yolks
Pinch of salt

In a small saucepan, slowly melt the butter over low heat. Remove the saucepan from the heat and gradually add the orange juice. Let stand for 5 minutes.

Beat the egg yolks lightly, and then beat a little of the yolks into the cooled butter mixture. Gradually dribble the butter mixture into the remaining egg yolks and blend well.

Return the mixture to the saucepan. Set over low heat and stir constantly until the sauce thickens. Serve immediately over the steamed asparagus.

Serves 2

COUS COUS

Although it's instant and from a box, cous cous served instead of white rice, bread, or even macaroni and cheese will make you look like the bon vivant you really are.

1 10-ounce package cous cous
Champagne
2 tablespoons chopped fresh mint leaves
(don't bother with the dried)

Prepare the cous cous according to package directions, substituting champagne for water or stock. When the cous cous is cooked, fold in the fresh mint leaves. Serve immediately.

Serves 2

THE "GO HOME!" BREAKFAST

Sometimes after a night or two of overnight guests, we wake up and the thrill is clearly gone. Suddenly the fog lifts and we see things for what they really are or, more important, what they should have been the night before. This newfound clarity is indeed refreshing, but the

MENU

Pancakes with
Roasted Pecans

Fresh Strawberries

Juice

Not Enough Coffee
and That's All!

situation remains. Still, there is no reason why this change of heart has to compromise the rest of your weekend. Part of being an expert host is knowing both how to welcome and how to say "Go Home," using the same inflection. Maybe your mother never addressed such issues as getting rid of overnight guests before 10 A.M., but I believe

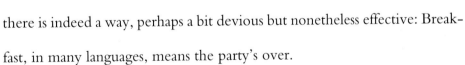

there is indeed a way, perhaps a bit devious but nonetheless effective: Breakfast, in many languages, means the party's over.

I'm not one to promote processed foods, but considering your exhaustion and urgency, using a mix might be an exception worth making. But, on the other hand, if you prepare pancakes from scratch, you will have more time alone in the kitchen. You can stand over the stove top promising that this will be the last time for more than one kind of mistake.

Roast a few pecans and toss on some fresh fruit and you can take this standard American breakfast and turn it into any omnivore's Last Supper. It will soften the inevitable impact of the words, "I have so much to do today, maybe I could call you." Given the circumstances, this meal is best not served in bed, but in the proximity of the front door. ∎

With practice, you'll be able to hustle your guest from wake-up call to the door in as little as 30 minutes, even if you start from scratch.

PANCAKES WITH ROASTED PECANS

When making pancakes either from scratch or a packaged mix, consider the first one or two as test pancakes. The first pancakes usually absorb the excess oil from the pan and are thus too soggy to eat.

2 cups all-purpose flour
3 teaspoons baking powder
$^1/_2$ teaspoon salt
2 eggs
$1^1/_4$ cups cold milk
$1^1/_2$ tablespoons sugar
1 teaspoon vanilla extract
1 teaspoon vegetable oil
Roasted Pecans (recipe follows)

Sift together the flour, baking powder, and salt. In a separate bowl, beat the eggs with the milk, sugar, and vanilla.

Pour the oil into a large skillet, then wipe with a paper towel, just to coat the skillet surface. Heat the skillet over medium high heat. When the oil starts to smoke a little, reduce the heat to medium. Pour enough batter into the center of the pan for your first pancake. When the batter in the center of the pancake bubbles, flip it over.

When browned on both sides and cooked through, remove from the pan and set aside on a plate in a warm oven. Repeat until you have used all the batter.

Serve with Roasted Pecans.

Serves 2

ROASTED PECANS

Use these to supplement your usual serving of maple syrup and save any leftovers for apple pie or ice cream.

2 teaspoons unsalted butter
1 cup pecan halves
$1/2$ teaspoon sugar
$1/4$ teaspoon cinnamon

Using the skillet in which you have just made the pancakes, first wiping away any excess crumbs or excess oil with a damp cloth, melt the butter over medium heat. Once the butter has melted add the pecans and toss to coat.

Sprinkle both the sugar and the cinnamon over the nuts and toss well, continue to cook, tossing frequently, until the nuts have darkened and the sugar has melted, or about 5 minutes.

Makes 1 cup

Pancakes speak louder than words, and more kindly, when you're ready to say "Go home!"

FOUR BIRTHDAY CAKES THAT WIN FRIENDS AND INFLUENCE PEOPLE

I enjoy birthdays mostly when they are not my own—when my advancing age is not the center of attention. One year I was taken to a small Mexican restaurant for a quiet dinner with three friends. When dessert arrived, a small pastry with a candle in it, everyone started

to sing—not just my table, but every other table, the waiters, the kitchen staff, and a few passersby on the street. I've been traumatized about birthdays ever since.

Generally when I know that it's someone's birthday I waste an inordinate amount of time prior to the actual event searching for the perfect gift (which I never

MENU

Carrot Cake

Chocolate Mousse Cake

"Guess Your Weight"
Ice Cream Cake

Harry's Birthday Cake

seem to find)—a gift that will stand out among all others. I waste so much time that the birthday usually passes unnoticed. Once again I have to somehow rescue another failed relationship. Birthdays just come and go too fast for me.

Given enough time, sometimes as little as a few hours, cakes present the perfect solution

for the hard-to-buy-for friend. A great-tasting cake with a little personality will be remembered long after all the gaudy neckties, ill-fitting sweaters, and Chia Pets have all found their way back to the store. So at the risk of sounding like a commercial for a long-distance phone company, memories are long-term gifts.

Each of the cakes here might take a little time and present a challenge, but with one of them and a good bottle of wine, you can show up three weeks or even a month after a birthday and still be regarded as a best friend. In fact, if baking birthday cakes turns out to be your only vehicle for entertaining, you will still find yourself at the center of a grateful social circle. ■

*Carrot Cake softens
the blow of
progressing age
with the illusion of
healthy living.*

CARROT CAKE

In this recipe the character of the traditional carrot cake is enriched by maple syrup so that it can be cut into smaller slices to feed the birthday masses. Use a syrup that actually says "Maple Syrup" on its label. Pancake syrup is seldom pure.

2 cups all-purpose flour
2 teaspoons baking soda
1 teaspoon salt
2 teaspoons cinnamon
1 teaspoon nutmeg
1¹/₂ cups sugar
1¹/₂ cups safflower oil
4 eggs
¹/₂ cup pure maple syrup
2 teaspoons vanilla extract
3 cups grated carrots
1 cup golden raisins
Cream Cheese Frosting (recipe follows)

Preheat the oven to 325° F. Butter and flour 2 8-inch cake pans.
Sift together the flour, baking soda, salt, cinnamon, and nutmeg. In a separate bowl, beat together the sugar, oil, eggs, maple syrup, and

vanilla. Blend the dry ingredients into the wet ingredients until smooth. Fold in the carrots and raisins.

Divide the batter evenly between the two prepared cake pans and bake on the middle rack of the oven for 50 to 55 minutes, or until cake tests done. (This means that when you're not really sure you stick the center with a toothpick. If it comes out dry, it's done.)

Let the cakes cool in the pans for 10 to 15 minutes. Then turn them out on a rack to finish cooling. When the cakes have cooled, frost them with Cream Cheese Frosting.

Serves 10 to 12

CREAM CHEESE FROSTING

1 pound (4 sticks) unsalted butter, at room temperature
1 pound cream cheese, at room temperature
2 pounds confectioner's sugar
4 teaspoons vanilla

Using an electric mixer on low speed and a large bowl, cream together the butter and cream cheese until well blended. Gradually add the sugar and vanilla and continue mixing on a low speed until frosting is smooth.

Frost the top of one layer of the carrot cake, position the second layer over it, and then frost the top and sides.

Makes enough for 1 cake

CHOCOLATE MOUSSE CAKE

This cake requires a bit of skill, but as long as you remember to fold instead of stir, you shouldn't have any problem. The operative pieces of equipment here are a large rubber spatula and a large metal bowl with shallow sides. Before you begin, chill the bowl in the freezer; this will increase the stability of the egg whites.

1 5^1/$_2$-ounce package shortbread cookies (see Note)
1 cup (8 ounces) semisweet chocolate
8 egg yolks, plus 10 egg whites
1^1/$_2$ teaspoons vanilla
^{1}/$_2$ cup sugar

Line the sides of an 8-inch springform pan with wax paper. Arrange 11 of the cookies vertically around the inside rim of the cake pan, trimming any irregular cookies carefully with a serrated knife so that they fit tightly. Set the pan aside.

In the top half of a double boiler set over simmering water, melt the chocolate in ^{1}/$_4$ cup water, stirring until smooth. Remove from the heat and let sit for 10 minutes. Fold in the egg yolks and vanilla.

In a separate bowl, beat the egg whites until foamy. Gradually add the sugar and continue beating until stiff peaks form. Stir a small amount of the egg white mixture into the chocolate mixture, then in three additions fold the rest of the egg whites into the chocolate mixture. Gently pour the batter into the prepared cake pan and chill for at least 4 hours.

Keep refrigerated until ready to serve. When ready to serve, carefully release the latch on the cake pan and remove the wax paper lining. Serve right from the cake pan base. Garnish with fresh berries, mint leaves, or whipped cream.

Makes one 8-inch cake

Note: I use Pepperidge Farm Old-Fashioned Shortbread Cookies because they fit perfectly into the pan.

*Before there was
Death and Taxes there
were Birthdays...
and Birthday Cakes—
Carrot Cake, above,
and Chocolate Mousse
Cake, right.*

NEW COLUMNS BY JIM HARRISON
Star-studded bash set for September . . .
'Slim or plump, she's my lady,' proclaims her steady beau
JAMES McCANDLISH
— Mickey Mansfield
Page 55

"GUESS YOUR WEIGHT" ICE CREAM CAKE

Serve this and watch any hopes of losing weight go down the drain in a chocolate blaze of glory. This is my answer to yogurt bars, fresh fruit, and anything made with granola. If frozen sufficiently, this cake can travel distances of up to 30 minutes away and then should be placed back in the freezer for another 30 minutes when you have reached your destination.

1½ boxes (13½ ounces) Famous Chocolate Wafers
½ cup (1 stick) unsalted butter, melted
1 pint each chocolate, vanilla, and coffee ice cream
1 cup heavy cream, whipped

Butter an 8-inch springform pan and set aside.
In a food processor reduce all of the wafers to crumbs. With the processor running, pour in the melted butter, then stop the machine. Firmly press the crumbs into the base and sides of the prepared cake pan and place the pan in the freezer.

Remove the chocolate ice cream from the freezer and let stand for about 20 minutes or until it is soft but not melted. In a large mixing bowl stir the ice cream with a spatula or a large wooden spoon until it is smooth. Pour the ice cream into the cake pan and smooth the top. Return the cake pan to the freezer for about an hour and a half.

Repeat these steps using the vanilla, then the coffee ice cream. Freeze the entire cake until ready to serve. To serve, release the latch on the cake pan and remove the ring. Top with the whipped cream and slice with a knife that has been warmed in hot water. Serve immediately.

Makes one 8-inch cake

Another diet sweetly bites the dust with the first bite of "Guess Your Weight" Ice Cream Cake.

HARRY'S BIRTHDAY CAKE

I make this every year for my friend Harry, hence the name. Essentially it is a large yellow cake filled with lemon mousse and topped with fresh whipped cream. It looks like it takes a bit of work, because it does. But it feeds about 12 people very generously and makes an incredible presentation. See picture on pages 116-117 for proof.

For the cake:
3 cups cake flour
2¹/₂ teaspoons baking powder
¹/₂ teaspoon salt
2 eggs
12 tablespoons (1¹/₂ sticks) butter, room
   temperature
1²/₃ cups sugar
2 teaspoons vanilla extract
1¹/₃ cups milk

For the mousse:
4 eggs, separated
³/₄ cup sugar
Juice of 1 lemon
Grated peel of 1 lemon

For the assembly:
2 cups seasonal berries, rinsed
2 cups heavy cream, whipped
4 or 5 wooden skewers

For the cake: Preheat the oven to 350° F. Butter and flour 2 8-inch springform cake pans.

Sift together the flour, baking powder, and salt. In another bowl, using an electric mixer, beat together the eggs, butter, sugar, and vanilla until creamy. Gradually add the milk and blend until smooth. Fold the flour mixture into the butter mixture until smooth.

Evenly divide the mixture between the two cake pans. Bake on the middle rack of the oven for 35 to 40 minutes or until cake tests done. Allow the cakes to cool in their pans for 10 to 15 minutes, then turn out on a rack to finish cooling.

For the mousse: In a medium bowl, beat the egg yolks with the sugar until smooth. Add the lemon juice and peel and stir.

In a double boiler, warm the lemon mixture over low heat until it thickens and coats the back of a spoon. Patience is required here. Do not let the lemon mixture boil. Remove from heat and allow to cool.

In a separate bowl, beat the egg whites until stiff but not dry, then fold the lemon mixture gradually into the egg whites in three additions. (Don't stir, or you'll collapse the whites.) Chill the mousse for at least 1 hour.

For the assembly: Slice both the cake layers in half horizontally. Spread a tablespoon of the mousse over the plate on which you plan to serve the cake. Place the first cake layer over that. Spread a third of the mousse over this layer. Top with another cake layer and another ¹/₃ of the mousse. Repeat this with the remaining cake layers and mousse, ending with the cake.

After securing the last layer, drive the skewers vertically into the cake to keep the layers from sliding. Cut off the tips of the skewers flush to the top of the cake. Top with the whipped cream and the berries. Chill until ready to serve.

Serves 12

WITH FRIENDS LIKE YOU, WHO NEEDS TIFFANY'S?

There was a time, all too recently, when my entertaining style had gotten out of hand, and I was dishing up elaborate dinners almost every week. Friends came to expect so much of me that they started to appear in formal dress bearing Rigaud candles, Peretti ashtrays, and

bottles of Dom Perignon. Gone were the T-shirts, jeans, and bouquets harvested from a neighbor's garden en route. I was appreciative, but concerned. Soon every night would become Academy Awards night, and I would be forever underdressed in my own home. I decided to take action.

MENU

Grilled Swordfish with Red Chili Mayonnaise

Simple Grilled Potatoes

Spinach Salad with Honey-Mustard Dressing

Rather than rent a tuxedo or hire a chamber ensemble, I invited the same overdressed and overburdened friends to dinner, but this time stressed the informality of the occasion. Supper, I reiterated, would be served in a seldom-visited corner of the backyard, the table setting would be everyday china, and the food would be embarrassingly rudimentary—fish, potatoes, and a store-bought dessert. No one exactly showed

up in overalls, but the mood was a lot less ostentatious. Since then, I've never turned back.

Every cook must learn when enough is enough. No matter how exalted your culinary reputation becomes, don't feel that every meal must be prepared with as much ceremony as if it were the Last Supper. Don't put the milk carton on the table—these are your friends, after all—but try to have as much fun as you did when you were too dumb to know any better. After all, if they hate the food, you can always bring out the vacation slides. ■

GRILLED SWORDFISH WITH RED CHILI MAYONNAISE

The simple marinade can be used on any kind of fish steak. Don't buy fish just because it's on sale. This usually means that it has been in the store too long and won't be fresh much longer.

4 tablespoons good olive oil
2 tablespoons lemon juice
3 tablespoons capers, drained and finely minced
1 teaspoon finely minced garlic
1 1-pound swordfish steak
Red Chili Mayonnaise (recipe follows)

In a small bowl whisk together the oil, lemon juice, capers, and garlic.

Place the fish in a shallow dish and pour the marinade over to cover. Chill, covered, for at least 30 minutes.

Prepare the grill as usual and allow the flames to die down and the coals to turn gray. Grill the fish about 5 minutes on each side, frequently brushing with the marinade. When the fish is grilled through, transfer it to a clean serving dish and discard any leftover marinade. Serve immediately.

Serves 3 to 4

Fast food doesn't have to mean dinner in a bag. Even the potatoes cook in under 20 minutes if the fire is hot enough.

RED CHILI MAYONNAISE

Mayonnaise is another food that is just as simple to make from scratch as it is to buy from the store. This mayo is made in the food processor in a few minutes and saves you from so many stabilizers, additives, and preservatives that you'll hardly notice the cholesterol.

1 egg
1 teaspoon lemon juice
Pinch of salt
1 tablespoon Dijon mustard
1 cup extra virgin olive oil
2 small red chili or hot peppers, seeded and finely minced

In a food processor using the chopping blade or in a blender, blend together the egg, lemon juice, salt, and mustard, and 1 tablespoon of the oil. Pulse the machine for about 30 seconds. With the machine running, slowly drizzle the remaining oil into the work bowl. Let the machine continue running until the oil has combined completely with the other ingredients, and the mixture starts to thicken.

Transfer the mayonnaise into a small mixing bowl. Fold in the chili peppers and chill for at least 2 hours. Homemade mayonnaise will last about four days in a very tightly sealed container in the refrigerator.

Makes about 1 cup

SIMPLE GRILLED POTATOES

It doesn't matter how adept you are with your barbecue tools, only Houdini could prevent at least one or two of these thinly sliced potatoes from meeting their demise in the fire. Do your best, and slice up extra potatoes if you are having a seriously clumsy day.

3 tablespoons unsalted butter
Salt and pepper
4 large Russet or Idaho
   potatoes, sliced $1/4$-inch
   thick lengthwise

Melt the butter in a small saucepan over low heat. Add salt and pepper to taste.

Brush the potato slices generously with the butter, and place on the grill. Cook until crispy, but not burned, on the outside and soft on the inside. Serve immediately.

Serves 4

....

**The entire meal can
be made, above,
and served, left,
in the backyard,
and any scraps
can be left for the
squirrels.**

SPINACH SALAD WITH HONEY-MUSTARD DRESSING

I like to use hydroponic spinach for salad. The leaves are flatter, so they don't trap as much grit as the curly, dirt-grown variety.

4 tablespoons extra virgin olive oil
1 tablespoon balsamic vinegar
1 teaspoon soy sauce
2 teaspoons honey mustard
1 pound fresh spinach leaves, rinsed, stems
   removed, and patted or spun dry
1 ripe tomato, cored and cut into wedges
8 ounces canned black beans, drained and
   rinsed well
1 ripe avocado, peeled and cut into wedges

In a small bowl, whisk together the olive oil, vinegar, soy sauce, and honey mustard until emulsified.

In a large bowl, toss the remaining ingredients with the dressing until well coated. Serve immediately.

Serves 6

REMEDIAL ENTERTAINING

Even with help some of us are slow learners. If you have tried a few meals and have not had the kind of success that would encourage you to open a restaurant, take heart. This menu is for you. While I cannot guarantee results, I can say that man does not live by Pudding Pops alone. We all must eat and, in turn, we all must cook. If it allays your anxiety, think of this as survival training instead of entertaining.

The rules are roughly the same as for scaling Mount Everest: Travel light and remember the basics. First: chicken. Always keep one or two three-pound whole chickens in the freezer. Defrost them in the refrigerator overnight. Next: instant wild rice and a one-step vegetable. Finally: stale bread returns as dessert. After a scant 30 minutes of preparation time, a fairly sophisticated dinner will emerge. (The chicken takes an hour to cook, but you'll be making the rest of the dinner while it is in the oven.)

If you practice this meal a few times, it will become as routine as a fire drill and a welcome replacement for your well-known bologna roll-ups. ◾

MENU

Honey-Baked Chicken

Fennel and Garlic

Wild Rice

Bread Pudding

HONEY-BAKED CHICKEN

Honey-Baked Chicken takes a high toll on whatever pan you might use. Lining the pan with aluminum foil is highly recommended.

1/4 cup honey
1/4 cup soy sauce
1/4 cup sesame oil
1 3–4 pound chicken, giblets removed, rinsed well and patted dry

In a small bowl whisk together the honey, soy sauce, and sesame oil. Place the chicken in a large plastic bag and pour the honey mixture over the chicken. Loosely seal the bag and place it in a large dish or bowl in the refrigerator for at least 2 hours. Turn the bag over a few times to evenly coat the chicken.

Preheat the oven to 400° F.

Take the chicken out of the bag and drain any excess marinade. Place the chicken on a rack in a roasting pan lined with foil. Bake for 1 hour without opening the oven door. Let the chicken stand for five minutes before serving. This is also delicious cold.

Serves 3 to 4

The delicious results of remedial entertaining are like passing the SATs of cuisine.

FENNEL AND GARLIC

I was not always a lover of fennel. This recipe is a treat for those stigmatized by less familiar greens or vegetables.

2 tablespoons unsalted butter
3 large garlic cloves, sliced
3 medium fennel bulbs, tops removed and cut into strips
1/2 cup dry white wine
Salt and pepper to taste

In a skillet over medium heat melt the butter, add the garlic slices, and sauté until lightly golden. Add the fennel and stir to coat well. Sauté for about 4 to 5 minutes. Gradually add the white wine and simmer for another 5 minutes. Serve immediately.

Serves 3 to 4

BREAD PUDDING

For some extra texture and a nutty flavor, a quarter cup of fresh pecans can be folded into the batter before pouring it into the baking dish. But it really is optional, as the top crust has a really great texture already.

3 tablespoons unsalted butter
1/2 cup lightly packed brown sugar
1 teaspoon baking soda
Pinch of salt
2 cups milk
1/4 teaspoon ground nutmeg
2 eggs
1 teaspoon vanilla
Dash of bourbon
4 cups stale whole wheat or white bread cubes

Preheat the oven to 350° F.

In a medium saucepan over low heat melt the butter. Add the brown sugar and cook until well blended and syrupy.

In a separate bowl, sift the baking soda and the salt into the milk. Gradually add this to the sugar mixture and sprinkle in the nutmeg. Then remove the saucepan from the heat and let stand 5 minutes.

In another bowl, whisk together the eggs and the vanilla. Blend some of the cooled milk and sugar mixture into the eggs, then add all of the eggs to the milk mixture and blend well. Stir in the bourbon. Fold in the bread cubes and stir well.

Pour the mixture evenly into a buttered 8 x 8-inch baking dish and bake for 45 minutes, or until the pudding has set and the top has browned. Let cool a bit and serve warm with whipped cream or with a splash of heavy cream.

Serves 6

Bread pudding is just as tasty as soufflé, and a lot easier on the nerves.

GOD IS MY SOUS CHEF

Growing up in a large Catholic family meant having fish for dinner one night every week. In our house, eating meat on Friday was punishable by the eternal fires of Hell or my grandmother's favorite threat: curvature of the spine. This was an all-purpose malady brought on

by a variety of offenses from the misdemeanors of picking one's nose and stealing from the collection plate to white-collar crimes like bribery or extortion. Clearly this was not just a hand-slap of nutritional information. The Vatican never addressed such controversial subjects as the importance of calcium in one's diet, so my brothers, sister, and I were forced to live with the fear that with one false bite we would never stand straight again, at least not without the assistance of a costly chiropractic device, countless novenas, or a sizable donation to the Church.

With this background, I am able to cook virtually any type of fish in any number of ways on any given day of the week. Although this isn't exactly the recipe we prepared every Friday in our house, it will guiltlessly serve both Catholics and pagans alike. ∎

MENU

Pan-Fried Fillet of Sole with Brana's Best Salsa

Sage Biscuits

Rice Stuffed Peppers

Vanilla Ice Cream with Blueberry Puree

PAN-FRIED FILLET OF SOLE

Fried slowly in about one half inch of oil, then well drained on paper towels, the fillets can be kept in a warm oven while you are preparing the rest of the meal.

2 eggs
3 dashes Tabasco sauce, or to taste
$1/4$ cup heavy cream
1 tablespoon Worcestershire sauce
1 cup cornmeal
1 cup all-purpose flour
1 teaspoon cumin
$1/2$ teaspoon red pepper flakes
2 tablespoons chopped fresh parsley
$1/2$ teaspoon salt
Vegetable oil
3 pounds fillet of lemon sole or flounder
Brana's Best Salsa (recipe follows)

In a 10-inch pie plate, gently beat the eggs. Add the Tabasco, the heavy cream, and the Worcestershire. In a large paper bag mix the cornmeal, flour, cumin, red pepper flakes, parsley, and salt. Seal the bag and shake.

Pour $1/2$ inch of vegetable oil into a deep skillet and heat over medium to high heat until drops of water sizzle. Keep the lid handy.

Rinse the fish well and dip each fillet in the egg mixture to coat, then into the bag with the flour mixture to coat well. Place the fish a few at a time in the hot oil, leaving enough room so that you can gently push them around as they are cooking to prevent them from sticking to the pan. Fry all of the fillets until they are crispy, flipping only once, about 6 minutes each side.

Remove to a paper towel to drain and keep warm in the oven until ready to serve with Brana's Best Salsa.

Serves 6

Sage Biscuits can also be used atop casseroles, alongside chili, or with afternoon tea.

BRANA'S BEST SALSA

My friend Brana is the reigning queen of remedial entertaining. She can make a complete supper out of whatever might be in her pantry, refrigerator, or the backseat of her car. She serves this salsa as a dip with tortilla chips, but I think it spices up life in general, especially fish.

2 cups seeded and chopped Italian plum
   tomatoes
1 4-ounce can peeled green chilies, drained
1 small yellow onion, chopped
1 garlic clove, finely minced
1 8-ounce can tomato sauce
2 tablespoons finely chopped fresh cilantro
Juice of 1 lime

In a small bowl combine all of the ingredients and blend well. Store covered in the refrigerator until ready to serve with the fish fillets.

Makes about 3 cups

SAGE BISCUITS

Any fresh or dried herb can be substituted for sage.

2 cups all-purpose flour
1 tablespoon baking powder
1 teaspoon salt
2 teaspoons finely chopped fresh sage, or $^1/_4$
   teaspoon dried
$^1/_3$ cup ($^2/_3$ stick) lightly salted butter, ice cold
   and cut into $^1/_2$-inch pieces
$^3/_4$ cup cold milk

Preheat the oven to 450° F.
In a large bowl, sift together the flour, baking powder, and salt. Blend in the fresh sage with a pastry blender, a fork, or clean hands, and mix in the butter until the mixture is crumbly. Gradually add just enough milk to make a coarse dough.

Roll out the dough on a well-floured surface to a $^1/_2$ - to $^3/_4$-inch thickness. Cut out biscuits with a floured 2-inch biscuit cutter or the floured top of a juice glass. Gather the scraps and roll out again.

Place the biscuits on an ungreased baking sheet and bake 10 to 12 minutes or until the biscuits have risen and their tops are golden. Remove to a rack to cool or serve immediately.

Makes about 2 dozen biscuits

Peppers before stuffing are a movable centerpiece, left. Blueberry puree is all ice cream needs to become dessert, above.

RICE STUFFED PEPPERS

Rice Stuffed Peppers are best when served in a variety of colors (red, yellow, and orange). I tend to stay away from the green ones, however, because, cooked, they are the greatest source of heartburn I know.

10 slices lean slab bacon
1 medium onion, chopped
1 garlic clove, finely chopped
2¹/₂ cups cooked white or brown rice
¹/₄ cup chopped fresh basil
¹/₂ cup dry white wine
4 medium bell peppers (assorted colors), cut
   in half lengthwise and seeded
Salt and pepper

Preheat the oven to 425° F.

In a skillet, fry the bacon until crisp. Transfer to a layer of paper towels to drain. Discard all but 1 tablespoon of bacon fat. Sauté the onion and garlic in the skillet until the onions are translucent. Remove the skillet from the heat. Crumble the drained bacon and return it to the skillet. Stir in the rice, basil, and half the wine. Stir well.

Generously fill the pepper halves with the rice and bacon mixture and place in a buttered baking dish. Pour the remaining wine over the pepper halves. Bake for 30 minutes, adding more wine if the peppers seem dry. Serve immediately.

Serves 4

VANILLA ICE CREAM WITH BLUEBERRY PUREE

···

In a few minutes you can whip up a great disguise for what is essentially a store-bought dessert.

2 tablespoons unsalted butter
$^1/_2$ cup sugar
$^1/_2$ teaspoon vanilla extract
1 pint fresh blueberries, rinsed and any
  stems removed
1 pint vanilla ice cream

In a saucepan over medium heat melt the butter. Add the sugar, vanilla, and blueberries. Cook until mixture is bubbly and the blueberries have softened. Remove the pan from the heat and let sit about 15 minutes.

Puree the mixture in a food processor, then strain. Serve while still warm over vanilla ice cream.

Serves 4

INDEX